"*Awakenings* challenges us to face the truth of it all and create anew. Such nourishment for our pluralistic and struggling world!"

— **Sister Simone Campbell**, SSS, executive director of Network Lobby for Catholic Social Justice

"An expansive vision for the Jewish American community, and it also helps us imagine what's possible across America's diverse religious landscape. This book is both pragmatic and hopeful, and it has a lot to offer readers of all backgrounds."

— **Simran Jeet Singh**, executive director for the Aspen Institute's Religion & Society Program and author of *The Light We Give*

"Rabbis Stanton and Spratt chart a course for Judaism and the Jewish community, showing us how to thrive in an increasingly globalized environment of hyphenated identities."

— **Calev Ben-David**, anchor of *The Rundown* on i24News

"Rabbis Stanton and Spratt skillfully remind us that the Jewish story is multifaceted in its scope and in its ability to influence society through its people. They help us to anticipate a growing Jewish identity that will draw upon its nuances and unique expressions to gain strength and vibrancy even in difficult times."

— **Bishop Robert Stearns**, founder and executive director of Eagles' Wings

"*Awakenings* brims with insight, gratitude, creativity, love, and stubborn hope. This hope is all the more compelling because it springs from a richly documented survey."

— **Matthew L. Skinner**, professor of New Testament at Luther Seminary

Rabbi Joshua Stanton • Rabbi Benjamin Spratt

Awakenings

American Jewish
Transformations in
Identity, Leadership,
and Belonging

Foreword by **Rev. Kaji Douša**,
Senior Pastor at Park Avenue
Christian Church

Afterword by **Dr. Eboo Patel**,
Founder and President of the
Interfaith Youth Core

BEHRMAN HOUSE
www.behrmanhouse.com

To our family, friends, teachers, and students who became
our teachers.
—J.S. & B.S.

Published by Behrman House, Inc.
Millburn, New Jersey 07041
www.behrmanhouse.com

ISBN 978-1-68115-089-5

Library of Congress Cataloging-in-Publication Data
Names: Stanton, Joshua, author. | Spratt, Benjamiń, author
Title: Awakenings : American Jewish transformations in identity,
    leadership, and belonging / by Rabbi Joshua Stanton and Rabbi Benjamin
    Spratt; foreword by Rev. Kaji Douša, Senior Pastor of Park
    Avenue Christian Church ; afterword by Dr. Eboo Patel, Founder and
    President of the Interfaith Youth Core.
Description: Millburn, New Jersey : Published by Behrman House, Inc., 2022.
    | Includes bibliographical references and index. | Summary: "An
    assessment of the challenges facing the American Jewish community, and a
    vision of this community's future"-- Provided by publisher.
Identifiers: LCCN 2021062178 | ISBN 9781681150895 (hardcover)
Subjects: LCSH: Jews--United States--Identity--21st century. | Jews--United
    States--Politics and government--21st century.
Classification: LCC DS143 .S67 2022 | DDC 305.89240973--dc23/eng/20220127
LC record available at https://lccn.loc.gov/2021062178

The publisher gratefully acknowledges Shutterstock or the following images: dove (cover and interior), parchment (cover), and sky (cover).

Design by Zatar Creative

Printed in China

9 8 7 6 5 4 3 2 1

Contents

Acknowledgments

We are filled with gratitude for our teachers, colleagues, contributors, readers, communities, friends, and families. There are countless people to thank, some of whom we are able to acknowledge here. David Behrman taught us how to write a book—and then agreed to publish it, along with his first-rate Behrman House team, including Vicki Weber, Dena Neusner, Alef Davis, and Diana Drew. Trena Keating of Union Literary did not represent us formally, but did show us the ropes and teach us much about what it meant to publish a book. We would never have met her without our friend Brian Platzer. Scholars Jonathan Sarna and Jack Wertheimer, along with early readers from among our families and circles of friends, provided important constructive criticism and suggestions for improvement of this manuscript. Dozens of colleagues and thought leaders gave of their time and wisdom through interview and reflection, invariably inspiring us with their generosity and vision. Our beloved communities at East End Temple, Congregation Rodeph Sholom in New York City, and Clal—The National Jewish Center for Learning and Leadership have done more for us than words can say. Each circle of community held space for us, taught us key lessons of leadership, gave us mentorship, and empowered us to take thoughtful risks, of which we hope this book is one. Lastly, our families did more than we could possibly have hoped to inspire us, give us time to write, and believe in what once seemed like a fanciful effort to compose a book together. Words cannot do justice to the love that we have received. Sincerely, thank you.

Authors' Note on Perspective

We are straight, white, cisgender men, fathers, and leaders who easily fit the archetype of the modern rabbi. We have stable jobs, serve vibrant congregations, do not have visible disabilities, and are beneficiaries of the status quo in the American Diaspora. We have been privileged in professional advancement, communal recognition, and financial remuneration.

Even from the limits of our field of vision, we witness a vast number of people ignored, silenced, or outright excluded from Jewish community experiences. And yet, even with (or even from) the pain of such experience, many of those cast to the margins of the American Diaspora hold the seeds of a new Jewish awakening. In this book, we do our utmost to elevate their wisdom, as well as the insights of many who seek positive change from places of power.

Foreword

We are in the middle of nothing short of an apocalypse.

It is not the first apocalypse, and it probably will not be the last. But an apocalypse is a cataclysmic ending to something. And *something* is ending.

The word apocalypse comes from the Greek ἀποκάλυψις (*apakalupsis*), where *apa* means "un-" and *kalupsis* means "cover." These "endings"—these apocalypses—actually *uncover* something. And there is much we need to uncover, including failures in individual leadership and even the failures of our beloved institutions.

This book is just that: an uncovering—an apocalypse of institution, revealing much we need to see and to grieve and to . . . awaken.

My neighbors Rabbis Spratt and Stanton call up this spirit of awakening. It is a revolutionary book for these apocalyptic times in a grieving nation that is saying goodbye to so much.

There is a reckoning pending this uncovering. But in the uncovering, in the revelation itself, the future unfolds to a beautiful awakening of just where God and goodness and beauty and faith and community can and must be. For such a time as this.

We cannot go back. Nor should we.

And as we move forward, we believe that we will do this, together.

Why on earth would two white rabbis ask a Black pastor to write the foreword to their book on a *Jewish* awakening? This is the question I asked Rabbis Ben and Josh in my living room on a recent stormy summer afternoon. In reading the manuscript, I knew that the book hit hard at cherished thinking *within* the Jewish community. Why bring in outsiders?

The answer is that cherished thinking needs a hard look *everywhere*. Particularly as we rightly orient our resources to protecting the good, to eliminating the poverty that need not exist, to eradicating the hatred that threatens *the very existence* of our people—we need to look, together. Blacks and Jews and those at the intersections therein will only survive and thrive with the survival and thriving of each other. So, of course, it makes sense that we will awaken, together.

Awakening together does not presuppose overlapping revelations. My own tradition within Christianity forcefully resists the heresy of super-sessionism. My vision of God does not need to compete with anyone else's. But our visions of God's justice *must* intersect.

Perhaps this is the new awakening people of faith require. Maybe this is what will be uncovered in these apocalyptic times. We do not know what is to come. But we can know—as this book so beautifully lays bare—that we are . . . becoming.

I thank the rabbis for taking this bold step to invite us all to "widen the aperture." As we do, watch the light come in.

Rev. Kaji Douša
Senior Pastor of Park Avenue Christian Church

Diaspora Aglow

Great disconnect between people and institutions suggests that we might not be standing at the cusp of a great assimilatory death spiral, but, rather, a Jewish awakening, wrought by the sense of individual empowerment that Jews—and the countless people connected to Jews or exploring Judaism—now feel.

At his inaugural address as president of the Jewish Theological Seminary of America, Solomon Schechter called for the widespread establishment of Jewish schools and places of learning across the United States.[1] Today, we bear witness to an American Judaism transformed by this vision. The Association of Jewish Studies now lists more than seventy-five departments of Jewish studies around the country, including most of the top universities in the world.[2] A total of 906 Jewish day schools now shape generations of emerging Jews,[3] and Judaism is now taught as a world religion in public high schools and colleges around the country.

Yet, just 120 years after Schechter's address, seminaries face existential peril—not because of failure, but because of their astounding successes. And they are not alone. Like many of the other institutions that helped strangers in a strange land find their footing, they face an obsolescence of their own making. The communities they fostered, equipped with modern leadership and taught to thrive in an American context, have outgrown the needs that the institutions were established to serve.

Our communal leaders, and more than a few prominent academics, fear that the death of long-standing organizations will mean the death of the American Diaspora itself. A narrative of Jewish self-destruction coalesced after the 1990 National Jewish Population Survey revealed that a growing number of Jews married someone who was not Jewish, waited to have children, had fewer children, were leaving Jewish population centers, and were not joining or were severing their ties to synagogues and other mainstays of Jewish life.[4] Jewish leaders and intellectuals interpreted the data in grim terms.

Literary critic and writer Leslie Fiedler likens intermarriage to a "silent Holocaust" in his 1991 compilation of essays *Fiedler on the Roof*:

> Not a single one of my own eight children has, at the present moment, a Jewish mate; nor for that matter do I. . . . In any case, there is no one to say kaddish for me when I die. I am, in short, not just as I have long known, a minimal Jew—my Judaism nearly nonexistent—but, as I have only recently become aware, a terminal one as well, the last of a four-thousand-year line. Yet, whatever regrets I may feel, I cannot deny that I have wanted this, worked for it.[5]

Many other communal leaders used the less incendiary expression "continuity crisis"[6] to describe how intermarriage would bring about the decline and fall of the American Diaspora.[7]

Today, this story continues to shape the way Jewish leaders view the American Diaspora. A *New York Times* headline from 2018 proclaims, "American Jews Face a Choice: Create Meaning or Fade Away,"[8] and the story goes on to explain five new books that affirm this premise. A contemporaneous piece in *Haaretz* argues, "Assimilation Is the Failure of American Jewry, Not Israel."[9] The BBC provides a slightly broader and more dispiriting picture, noting, "As today's rate of intermarriage among Diaspora Jews stands above 50 percent, many are worried that the nation that survived persecution, pogroms, and the Holocaust could eventually die out of its own undoing."[10] Even Israeli leaders are weighing in publicly. As one headline notes, "Israeli Minister Says US Jews Marrying Non-Jews Is 'Like a Second Holocaust.'"[11]

Alan Dershowitz's book *The Vanishing American Jew* sums up this mindset:

> American Jewish life is in danger of disappearing, just as most American Jews have achieved everything we ever wanted: acceptance, influence, affluence, equality. As the result of skyrocketing

rates of intermarriage and assimilation, as well as "the lowest birth rate of any religious or ethnic community in the United States," the era of enormous Jewish influence on American life may soon be coming to an end.[12]

The narrative is simple and compelling. If Jews do not partake in organized Jewish life, that signals a failure of wayward individuals, not organizations. Jews don't learn anymore. They don't pray anymore. They don't marry fellow Jews anymore. They don't have enough children anymore. They don't raise their children Jewishly enough anymore.

Rather than probing in detail why institutions are not serving the needs of an increasingly integrated American Diaspora, pundits, academics, and community leaders focus on a presumptive cause and convenient bogeyman: assimilation. Unless genetic Jews marry other genetic Jews and have lots of genetically Jewish babies, then synagogues, federations, seminaries, and our entire Jewish way of life is on its way out. The proposed remedy has been a series of interventions to keep Jews marrying Jews and to bring the unaffiliated back into membership in a synagogue or communal organization.[13] With the majority of Jews disconnected from *any* institution, this trend has not been interpreted as a symptom of disaffection with those organizations, as much as a rejection of Judaism itself.

This story of woe is not a new one. As captured succinctly by historian Jonathan Sarna, "Regularly, American Jews hear, as I did at the start of my career from a scholar at a distinguished rabbinical seminary—and as other Jews did in colonial times, and in the era of the American Revolution, and in the nineteenth century, and in the twentieth century—that Judaism in America is doomed."[14]

Our obsession with the narrative of decline overlooks threads of optimism and opportunity. The comfort of this well-worn story anchors us to past generations' angst. We feel the inevitability of failure, even when much is going well. We are still just a fiddler on the roof, destined to come crashing down at some point.

And we can find support for this dire view in real experience and data. Intermarriage continues to rise. Many of the institutions that defined American Judaism for the past century have been declining or disappearing. Many of our Jewish leaders fall in stature and influence as antisemitism rises.

But all this grounds our attention in a past that may not be prologue and ignores fundamental changes in Judaism's place within American society. And when we widen the aperture of our lens, we may see another story, a new narrative, woven within this familiar casting of the Jewish continuity crisis.

The number of Americans who self-identify as Jewish is growing rapidly—from 5 million to 7.5 million people since 1990.[15] New institutions, initiatives, and Jewish identities continue to emerge. Upcoming generations redefine roles and structures of power, spreading centralized power into networks of impact. In opening this broader lens of understanding our Diaspora, we see a Judaism filled with transformations and the bloom of possibility, amid the collapse of comfort. Our Diaspora brims with dynamism.

Even as self-identified American Jews leave mainstream Jewish organizations, they exude pride of identity[16] and new ways to express it. This great disconnect between people and institutions suggests that we might be standing at the cusp not of a great assimilatory death spiral but rather of a Jewish awakening, wrought by the sense of individual empowerment that Jews—and the countless people connected to Jews or exploring Judaism—now feel.

In the twenty-first century, American Jews hold more wealth, access, and power in larger society than in any Diaspora of the past three millennia. Jews run for president, lead industry, create new fields of study, and shape law and policy, while Jewish culture captivates society through television, comedy, music, and art. Rather than the narrative of the resilient underdog, the story of the modern American Jew is one of potency and choice.[17]

Jews were long downtrodden and stateless. Now most are free and equal citizens in the most vibrant Diaspora in our history, while a reborn State of Israel blossoms.[18] Even as American Jews face ongoing tribulations from antisemitism,[19] national surveys over the past decade also report that American Jews are consistently the best-liked and most well-respected religious community in the United States.[20]

We still feel the immense momentum of people, power, and purse to return our people to the Land of Israel, acculturate in America, and ensure the security of both populations. Yet, in an era when Israel wields military and economic might like no rival in the region and Jews make up a growing portion of America's power brokers, these missions feel increasingly out of touch with the needs of our people.

In the wake of these successes, American Jewish institutions have been left with a vacuum of new purpose, defending existing achievements and defaulting to past tropes. The American Diaspora needs a new unifying vision, as a network of individuals harnesses Jewish tradition to realize the human power for good in an increasingly complicated and fractured world. We are on the cusp of a Jewish awakening, inspired by Jewish practice but open to all.

Thousands of people join Judaism every year across the country as Jews by Choice, while hundreds of thousands more live with Jews or as Jews without formal conversion. American Judaism is finally beginning to acknowledge the hundreds of thousands of Jews of Color who had been undercounted in population studies.[21] Nearly 60 percent of children with only one Jewish parent are raised as Jews, and an even larger majority are exposed to Judaism.[22]

New possibilities abound. Lines of leadership are being redrawn, with clergy ceding power to a broadening cohort of Jewish professionals and lay leaders. Technology is enabling us to explore the possibility of communities based on shared interests and values, rather than shared neighborhoods. Ongoing efforts could enable pluralism to overtake denominationalism and create spaces for people who range from open-minded ultra-Orthodox to hyphenated heterodox to learn, grow, and explore Jewishly together.[23] Israel can engage with the American Diaspora as a respected peer, rather than a vulnerable dependent.

American Jewish communal institutions are changing at an unprecedented rate. Synagogues, community centers, federations, advocacy organizations, and seminaries once served as liaisons between Jewish and American identities. Some now face a loss of purpose, while many are racing to identify and adapt to the new needs of the people whom they seek to serve.

Nigel Savage, the former chief executive officer of Hazon, reflected:

> The organizational map of American Jewish life reflected the psychic needs of American Jews from the 1930s to 1970s or 1980s. It worked. Then, at a certain point, the map didn't work anymore. Literally, both physical buildings and the culture of religious institutions moved slower than the current culture. It created a mismatch that has described the last twenty-five to thirty years.[24]

This mismatch between American Jewish needs and the offerings of American Jewish institutions has triggered a new expansion of the American Jewish story. Jewish start-ups have burst forth into the mainstream, disrupting notions of community, philanthropy, advocacy, spirituality, learning, and belonging. Some are already scaling up to compete with long-standing bastions of American Judaism, which themselves were once start-ups.

Urban geographer Elissa Sampson has drawn parallels between this moment of empowerment and that of German American Jews in the late nineteenth century, who used their upward mobility to found important institutions with three driving purposes: to ameliorate the condition of Jews across Eastern Europe, to acculturate those who emigrated to the United States, and to create a unifying sense of belonging. The success of these institutions also amplified the disparity between Ashkenazic Jews and other American Jewish communities. In response, Eastern European Jews went on to found their own communal institutions to better serve their communities as they became the majority of US Jews. Spiritual entrepreneur Rabbi Elan Babchuck has likened our own time to the pivotal decades from the 1880s through the 1920s that birthed many of the mainstays of American Jewish life that we know—and perhaps even take for granted—today.[25]

Historian Jonathan Sarna identified a similar period spanning the turn of the twentieth century as a "Jewish awakening," with a "bottom up" religious revival, new leadership, the empowerment of women, renewal of Jewish learning and scholarship, and the formation of intellectual circles and publications.[26] Some of the decentralized leadership of this key historical period in American Jewish life focused on revitalizing the Land of Israel; others on the rise of Jews within American society; still others on the role American Jewry could play as a beacon to Jewish communities around the world; still more on intellectualism and forward-looking Jewish ideas, as well as the publications that promoted those ideas.

Many of the organizations that coalesced over a century ago continue to take center stage today. They rose from the grass roots, bringing forward the spirit of revival from the individual to the communal and on to the national web of relationships composing an interconnected Diaspora.

The United Jewish Appeal and Jewish Federation joined forces and pioneered federated giving of the sort that became part of the American social fabric. The American Jewish Committee set the stage for modern religious diplomacy. The Anti-Defamation League broke new ground in protecting Jews—and countless other groups—from prejudice, discrimination, and hatred. The National Council of Jewish Women centered women in Jewish life and leadership. Synagogues created space for new immigrants and helped them formulate authentically Jewish and American expressions of identity. Prayer books united communities in modes, melodies, and expressions of worship. New seminaries trained a rising generation of religious leaders. Denominations experimented with American and Americanizing modes of Jewish community and practice. Our Diaspora has succeeded beyond its wildest dreams because of the path that these and numerous other institutions carved for American Jews.

It has been more than a hundred years since we last witnessed such a vast reimagining of Jewish life, when wave upon wave of immigrants from Eastern Europe arrived in our country. American Jews have clearly realized the early goals of the prior awakening.

Within the present resides the promise of another Jewish revival. Jews—and potential Jews and people who are Jewishly connected and those who are Jewishly curious—are hungry for new expressions of spirituality, values, and community. Grassroots leadership is springing up around us as external manifestations of internal transformations.

This book charts some of the dynamics at play from a place of hope about the future, while acknowledging the sense of disequilibrium and loss that rapid change engenders. It seeks to create a new narrative that is both forthright and compassionate to all who are connected to the American Diaspora, including millions of people who do not identify as Jews and the coming generations who understand Jewish identity in different terms than did their immigrant forebears. It challenges the dual assumptions of a Jewish continuity crisis and institutional obsolescence, noting the extent to which legacy institutions can incubate the future, while start-ups and mission-focused initiatives can collaborate to shape movements or grow into major institutions. It also charts a new path for rabbis, cantors, and other Jewish clergy as spiritual entrepreneurs, connectors, and idea generators.

Our hope is not to map in detail what is yet to come, so much as to identify the dynamics and forces at work that may shape the future of the American

Diaspora and could lead to profound spiritual gains for our community. We delve into the underpinnings of narratives that are too simple on the surface to help us comprehend the upside of all that is before us in the American Diaspora. We draw from Torah, Jewish history, best practices from business and other sectors, and dozens of interviews with thought leaders from across denominations, including executives of American Jewish institutions, laypeople, and innovators in other traditions.

This book comes to the unsurprising conclusion that our past in the American Diaspora was far less idyllic than the narratives we often tell ourselves and that the future holds far more promise than we allow ourselves to imagine. If there is an enduring gift from our tradition of debate and reexamination, it is the ability to hold complexity with care and as a necessary source of wisdom.

As we draw on the complexity of the American Jewish past, we note the trends of change today. These trends provide the hopeful basis for growth in the depth and breadth of experiences that we can provide in the American Diaspora. They also call into question the narrative of continual collapse, which, in addition to being undermined by new data,[27] overlooks the possibility of becoming a home for the spiritually disenfranchised,[28] who have become disaffected with the religious traditions in which they were raised. By redoubling best practices, we can connect with the tens of millions of Americans seeking a framework by which to lead purposeful, ethical, and joyful lives.[29] We can also strengthen the moral fiber of American society by sharing with more people Jewish intellectual, spiritual, and social practices, without any conversionary intent.

To do so, we need to move beyond narratives that came into being when we were a socially marginalized, immigrant community, defined externally by majority culture. We can choose to see hyphenated identities as an opportunity to enrich the Jewish community, rather than a sign of threat or failure. We can choose to see the pace of technological and social change as an opportunity for experimentation, growth, and new leadership, rather than an indication of erosion or erasure. We can choose to view synagogues, Jewish community centers, and Hillel as more than havens from wider society, but also as centers for spiritual development and outreach. As Aviva Zucker Snyder of Hillel International puts it, it's about helping more people engage in "active Jewish self-authorship and feeling pride in who they are."

We also call into question the dichotomy of "legacy" and "start-up" institutions, affirming that both mainstay organizations and newcomers are essential to the creative process of the American Diaspora—and that many organizations at the core of Jewish life today were once start-ups. In intentionally linking multiple stages in the organizational life cycle, we may ensure that they complement one another with stability and flexibility, tradition and innovation.

Synagogues could grow into national franchises, based on unique brands and offerings, as geographic monopolies fall away and technology buttresses connection from afar. The Jewish Federation system could continue growing as an exemplar of philanthropic giving and an incubator of Jewish social ventures.

At the same time, mission-driven start-ups may begin to coalesce into communities of belonging, based around key areas of purpose and action. Cutting-edge communities in the Jewish Emergent Network already do precisely this, focusing on specific values or areas of interest that together compose a rubric of community life, inspired by dynamic clergy and communal worship.[30] People come with a purpose but stay because of their growing sense of belonging, rather than the other way around.

In some respects, this era might mark a renewal of classical forms of learning and spiritual practices, as well as the adaptation of successful strategies from American Orthodox communities.[31] Chasidic mindfulness practices and ethical practices of *tikun midot* are centuries old and are making a comeback through the Institute for Jewish Spirituality, the Mussar Institute, and synagogues across the country. Houses of study are springing up from participants in and alumni of the Hadar Institute, the Pardes Institute of Jewish Studies, the Shalom Hartman Institute, and countless other intensive learning programs, normalizing the discursive study of Jewish texts in religious schools, on college campuses, and through adult education courses. As Rabbi Leon Morris, president of the Pardes Institute, reflected, "If we are to take a Jewish institution from antiquity, it should be the *beit midrash* [house of study]. American Jews are skeptical, anti-dogmatic, and highly intellectual. They love reading, arguing, and discussing."[32]

An era of experimentation, growth, and adaptation has given more Jewishly connected people more space to articulate purposes that can unite the American Diaspora. Technology is providing more ways to reach more people, without supplanting the fundamental human need to be together in person. A multiracial, multigender, polythetic,[33] self-actualized Diaspora awaits us, as we center human needs and recognize that our people can no longer be defined by genetics as much as by continual self-improvement through intentional practice, community support, and a belief in our higher purpose.

As we witness the seismic shifts continuing around us, we hear a societal cry for connection and wellness. We may draw on the wisdom of our Babylonian sages, who shifted a sense of singular Temple into the technology of *chavruta* (learning through partnered fellowship) and minyan. They imagined that God would dwell in the connections of people more than the construction of institutions and that the sacred altars of the dining table would offer soulful dialogue in place of priestly sacrifice. The long arc of Jewish history affords us the blessing to see a familiar shift toward decentralization gaining strength once again.

Emblazoned on the proud entranceway of the Jewish Theological Seminary of America are the enduring words of wonder about the burning bush. Even fully ablaze, "the bush was not consumed."[34] The bush is glowing in new colors today. A longer gaze and a broader view show us what makes it wondrous: the fires do not consume it, but transform it into a beacon of purpose. We need only awaken to its brilliance and empower more people to behold it with wonder.

PART 1

Purpose Petrified

The blessings of integration that contemporary Jews experience are testament to the success of countless organizations and the generations of leaders who drove them. The initial purposes that inspired much of the American Jewish infrastructure have been achieved, and these same institutions are now falling victim to their own success. An emphasis on nostalgia and authenticity encourages us to mythologize the past and narrow our awareness of the present. A focus on buildings and centralized power by much of American Judaism reflects the realities of a century ago. In understanding what keeps these organizations mired in the past, we can unearth a new purpose to unify the American Diaspora and guide it toward a new golden age.

CHAPTER 1

Peddling Nostalgia as Salvation

The stories we tell about our past shape our future.

Following the Exodus from Egypt, the Israelites wander in the wilderness and face new lands and new struggle. They repeatedly decry their departure from Egypt and laud their days of slavery: "Why have you brought God's congregation into this wilderness for us and our beasts to die there? Why did you make us leave Egypt to bring us to this wretched place, a place with no grain or figs or vines or pomegranates? There is not even water to drink!"[1] If even bondage in Egypt can give rise to sweet memories, imagine how much we distort more mundane recollections of the past with our nostalgia.

In 2016, the Public Religion Research Institute found that 51 percent of the US population felt that the American way of life and culture had changed for the worse since 1950.[2] The majority of the country moved from reaching toward the "American Dream" back toward memories of the American past. Psychologically, this kind of nostalgia can help us cope with moments of deep uncertainty and discontinuity. It enables us to sidestep present realities and invites us into a familiar past that can restore esteem and confidence.

Researchers have found that nostalgia can increase feelings of social connectedness and a sense of meaning in life.[3] We may feel anchored in love and relationship, sense belonging and comfort, and view remembrance as a return to the "good old days." As captured succinctly by Edoardo Campanella and Marta Dassù, "Yesterday is associated with progress, tomorrow with stasis or regression."[4] Today, nostalgia continues to take on far too much prominence in the way we conceive of the American Diaspora.

From the heights of academia, first at Stanford University's Jewish Studies Department and then as chancellor of the Jewish Theological Seminary of America, Dr. Arnold Eisen considers Jewish nostalgia as a form of obligation we, as American Jews, owe to our forebears: "To carry on an observance from one's parents is to make them live in and through that observance. . . . To abandon Judaism is, in that psychological sense, to kill the parents/ancestors, by losing touch with what they had stood for and done."[5] Eisen sees the nostalgic gaze as a lens of meaning-making for the modern Jew. The melancholy and sense of displacement, inherent in nostalgia, unsettle the modern Jew from present-day comforts in order to remain emotionally invested in the past.

From Chabad to Aish HaTorah, Larry David's borscht belt humor, the Kabbalah Centre, and fundraising campaigns to secure Israel and boost membership in synagogues and communal organizations, most of our organizations rely on nostalgia to garner support and instill a sense of purpose. Liturgy becomes the litmus test of legitimacy, Hebrew a signal of authenticity, and the Polish garb of Ashkenazic ultra-Orthodoxy a sign of authority. Nostalgia rests on a belief in the "good old days," a sense that with time we distance ourselves from better versions of ourselves and our world. Such a lens positions synagogues as gateways to the Jewish past and religious rituals as inviolate anchors of our people. It inspires philanthropy, keeps clergy employed, and amplifies a purpose that centers on the retrospective as our only counter to the changes inherent in the flow of time.

Even trendier aspects of Jewish culture and life have come to root themselves in nostalgia, including more than a few restaurants and delis. In 2010, Noah Bernamoff and Joel Tietolman founded Mile End Deli in Brooklyn, New York, naming the restaurant after the Jewish immigrant neighborhood in their hometown of Montreal. As Bernamoff writes in *The Mile End Cookbook*, he originally sought to bring Montreal cuisine to those hankering for a good meal. But with the death of his grandmother, his vision evolved:

> This woman was the glue that held my family together. And the reason my family happily allowed themselves to be glued was Nana Lee's food. Her food, and her huge Friday-night dinners, gave structure and substance to our lives. . . . Maybe I overreacted, but

when she died, I thought to myself: Is this the end? Will this food find someplace to live on in our lives? Suddenly everything shifted into focus. This restaurant we were about to open had to be a Jewish restaurant.[6]

These are the very questions that underpin so much of modern American Jewish identity. Familiar flavors, the sounds of *Mizrachi* melody or Yiddish idiom—all these may capture the modern Jewish psyche by conveniently entwining authenticity, comfort, and rootedness for those seeking place and purpose. At the same time, such a nostalgic gaze may invite a resolution to deeper existential fears. In touting the best of what was, we declare that our lives are more than mere memory that fades over time. The taste of borscht, the sound of Kol Nidrei,[7] the wine-stained Haggadah[8] become totems of immortality and icons of a mythic past. The nostalgic gaze bestows upon us the illusion of place and purpose.

Nostalgia's power also involves a necessary forgetting, a welcome amnesia that enables us to gloss over the realities of the past. In our delight over reclaiming borscht, we may ignore the poverty that necessitated such culinary invention. As millions of Jews still feel moved by the Kol Nidrei prayer, we may forget both what first inspired it and also the centuries of animosity and controversy this prayer, in turn, inspired. "Tradition" simply marks the moments when change powerfully took hold, with a concomitant forgetting of both the struggle and the change itself.

We may forget the scarcity that forced our culinary creativity,[9] the persecution to which mournful cantorial flourishes point,[10] and the poverty, mortality rates, ignorance, and racism of bygone ages, all nested within mythic remembrances of shtetl life.[11] The present power of Jews in the fields of medicine, politics, law, and media all grew out of the very scarcity of such power in prior generations. Icons like the Harmonie Club indeed helped inspire a renaissance of American Jewish culture but emerged out of necessity from discrimination and social marginalization.[12]

Nostalgia's consecration of the backward gaze may also limit our vision of the future and diminish our sense of responsibility for the challenges of the present. Nostalgia views waning synagogue attendance as the rejection of ancestry and authenticity, rather than a signal of needed change in mode and purpose. It echoes the rhetoric of "Jewish continuity crisis,"[13] which prioritizes endogamy over partnering for love and ignores the far more complicated question of how we can enable more people to find meaning in Jewish ritual, ideas, community, or experience. Nostalgia lives at the heart of scare tactics that liken intermarriage to the Holocaust[14] and changes in Jewish behavior and ritual to a desecration of our past.

The emotional blackmail of threatening not to attend interfaith partnership ceremonies or even the severing of a parent-child relationship transcends denomination and leads to a cycle of insecurity about who is Jewish "enough." Ultra-Orthodox Jews marrying across sects might meet the same parental opprobrium as a Reform Jew raising children with a secular humanist of non-Jewish ancestry.

The nostalgic gaze tells the story of decline and distance, rather than of a vibrant future. Rabbi Abraham Joshua Heschel, the great public theologian of our Diaspora, identified this problem decades ago in his work *Man Is Not Alone* and enjoined American Jews to pursue an identity that is more than the retrospective:

> To have faith does not mean, however, to dwell in the shadow of old ideas conceived by prophets and sages, to live off an inherited estate of doctrines and dogmas. In the realm of spirit only he who is a pioneer is able to be an heir. The wages of spiritual plagiarism are the loss of integrity; self-aggrandizement is self-betrayal. Authentic faith is more than an echo of a tradition. It is a creative situation, an event.[15]

Some of us may be quick to gild the glory days, while others may tear down the statues of former failures. But both paths preclude the possibility of a usable past, a past that tells the complicated story of how we have grown and may continue to grow. It is this wide-open lens that may come to shape a new Jewish awakening, in which our past fuels our drive to create the future.

We may tell the story of founding fathers as saintly, visionary heroes or as racist slave owners—or, instead, as complex leaders whose courage was sometimes overshadowed by human failings, giving us the opportunity to be even better. Abraham, the great father to many nations, is also the one willing to abandon one son and sacrifice the other. We bear witness to Sarah's laughter and Hannah's prayer in the face of infertility. We see a thriving Diaspora that came to the fore two millennia after the destruction of the Second Temple in Jerusalem. The stories we tell about our past shape our future. Even the artifacts of memory, studied with care, can inspire a powerful, forward-looking trajectory.

When Senator Jon Ossoff, the first Jewish US senator from Georgia, was sworn in on January 20, 2021, he carried in his jacket pocket copies of the manifests for the ship his great-grandparents were traveling aboard when they arrived at Ellis Island. This act elevated his election to a larger story of Jewish belonging and Jewish power in America, tying the legacy of his immigrant ancestors to his present political position. For Senator Ossoff, these photocopies suggested that the past might inspire a present purpose, orienting the past to serve our sought-after future. In his own words:

> I think that Jews share a story that compels us to approach the world with empathy. Because our story is one of hardship, persecution, perseverance—our story is one which has required us to fight for our freedom and survival, which has required us to find those of other faiths who, with kindness and empathy, have harbored us at other times of great danger. Most Jews, no matter where they live in the world, share an immigrant story. We have been a people on the move. That heritage informs my commitment to a vision of America that is open and decent, kind and respectful. That lives up to our national character as a place that welcomes strivers from afar and those fleeing violence and persecution.[16]

This is not the melancholy gaze toward a mythic past, but rather a sense of the past that breeds purpose and resolve. It represents neither the abandonment of ancestry nor a sense that Jewish identity hinges on nostalgia. Senator Ossoff did not anchor his political career in the past as much as trace it to the past and use that to identify a north star and a path yet to be determined. However we may feel about his politics, he, too, is emblematic of the Jewish awakening.

CHAPTER 2

The Authenticity Trap

Giving primacy to authenticity traps power and
belonging in the space of the few and the privileged.
In dismantling this trap, we can extend power and
belonging to all who seek it.

We typically link the "traditional" with a sense of the "authentic" or "genuine." But doing so also requires rejecting the possibility that change is inherent in tradition.[1] Mourners in our communities demand that clergy bury people the "right way," when they have never before observed any traditional Jewish practices. Brides circle grooms seven times in a ritual that is rarely understood, even as it echoes ancient patriarchal attitudes.[2] In the sweltering heat of summer, Chasidic Jews in Dallas dress in the warm clothing of their brethren from the seventeenth-century Pale of Settlement, even though none of our ancient ancestors described in the Torah wore anything of the sort.[3] Centuries of rabbis have attempted to eliminate the Kol Nidrei prayer from erev Yom Kippur services or to alter it, only to repeatedly discover that the experience of the prayer is the anchor of authenticity for many Jews.[4]

Intermarried LGBTQ people may still donate to Aish HaTorah and seek "true" blessing from Chasidic rabbis, even though the organization might reject many layers of their identity. Celebrations of *b'nei mitzvah* have become an industry, focusing on gaudy parties, rather than an affirmation of heritage and humanity. The bereavement ritual of sitting shiva has inspired its own digital platforms, as websites like shiva.com delineate authentic mourning practices so mourners and comforters alike follow proper scripts and behaviors.[5] Those seeking magical expressions of Judaism can buy protective talismans and healing cups, purported to be blessed by rabbis and imbued with kabbalistic power.[6]

The challenge here is that this yearning for authenticity is both mythic and binding. "Judaism" and "Jewishness" have existed in so many different eras and places that even the concept of "Jewish authenticity" limits our scope and gives precedence to the simple over the nuanced. The pendulum swings of decay and innovation, of constancy and change, and of assimilation into and out of Judaism are so pervasive that the most authentic path may be to embrace potential inauthenticity.[7] The act of learning, of illuminating the contexts and conflicts of our Jewish past, deepens the connectivity of Judaism within a larger world and empowers us to shape our response to it as individuals.

Our worship at the altar of nostalgia merits attention. For therein lies a corollary to peddling nostalgia as salvation: the trap of authenticity. In mythologizing the look and sound of a "real" Jew, we diminish the depth and diversity of Judaism and circumscribe Jewishness, giving it a narrow focus. Who is more authentic—the Sephardic Floridian or the Ashkenazic Californian or the New York Jew by Choice? Is it more authentic to gamble with a dreidel on Hanukkah, despite millennia of prohibitions against gambling, or for a bat mitzvah to chant from the Torah, despite the taboo against such female-identified leadership for much of Jewish history? Is a German drinking song[8] a more authentic melody for the hymn Adon Olam than "Take Me Out to the Ballgame"?

The authenticity game may be a trap that encourages myopia and sidesteps the inherent complexity and remixings found throughout Jewish history. It bolsters the identity of the few at the cost of belonging for so many others, and while it plays into the insecurities of modern American Judaism, it does so by viewing Judaism through a selective, retrospective gaze.

When Rabbi Mordecai Kaplan published *Judaism as a Civilization* in 1934 and evoked the "contemporary crisis in Jewish life," he was referring to institutions that did not meet the needs of the community they served. That those same institutions are still around today is a testament to vested interests.

When examining the stasis of many Jewish institutions over a century of dramatic change in America, one must note who benefits from the status quo. It is those with the most accumulated privilege. In 2017 every single one of the top twenty-eight paid Jewish nonprofit executives were men,[9] and in 2021 men lead sixteen of the seventeen largest Jewish federations.[10] According to the Reform Pay Equity Initiative, women still earn just four-fifths of what their male counterparts do within Jewish institutions.[11] Rabbis are the highest-paid clergy in America.[12]

Yet, as the myth of the "sage on a stage" continues to fade and the doors of outdated institutions close, the allure of authenticity at the expense of empowerment will wane. Ultimately, a broader definition of authentic connection to Jewish tradition may enable our Diaspora to realize its potential. A return to the era of the early rabbis may be afoot, in which we all learn and teach, pray and gather, lead and reimagine. The distinctions between lay leader and clergy, institution and network, are already beginning to blur.

We may all be students of Torah. The majesty of our tradition is the process of learning from it and practicing it, not possessing it and claiming to speak in its name. Community is built by people who seek to grow in spiritual collaboration. In the words of Moses himself, "Would that all of God's people were prophets."[13] Authenticity limits power and belonging to the space of the few and the privileged; in dismantling such a limit, we may extend such power and belonging to all who seek it.

CHAPTER 3

Edifice Rex

> Our communities pay an extraordinary price for these
> awe-inspiring and disempowering spaces, which divert
> resources from the human-centered projects of our
> community's future.

O ur communal spaces make us feel safe and at home, fill us with awe, and connect us to the past. They can affirm the beauty of our faith and imagine more fully the glory of the historic pilgrimages to a central Temple in Jerusalem. They embody our virtues and help us remember that while Jewish life is about obligation, it is also about beauty, joy, and a shared sense of place.

Yet our spaces can also snare us in nostalgia for a time when we were just barely "making it" in America. The booming voice of the rabbi must come from a correspondingly grand pulpit. When sitting in a cavernous synagogue sanctuary, we feel like a small part of it, rather than an individual empowered to learn and lead within our community. Our communities pay an extraordinary price for these awe-inspiring and disempowering spaces, which divert resources from the human-centered projects of our community's future. Indeed, buildings are another manifestation of our petrified purpose. The resources, time, and energy devoted to building and maintaining them both sap the vitality of the organization and show the extent to which our communities no longer are mission-driven.

Building campaigns dot the American Jewish landscape, with countless opportunities for major donors to emblazon their names upon synagogue, day school, federation, and organizational buildings. Some of these campaigns collect tens or even hundreds of millions of dollars for cathedrals to our Diaspora's ascendance.[1] They represent its financial comfort, its embrace of norms set by American universities, and, yes, those set by American churches. These buildings symbolize our Diaspora's permanent presence. They also belie our lack of focus on a higher purpose our community should serve. Our obsession with physical space, alongside a waning affiliation of those wishing to pay for access to such space, illustrates the extent to which many institutions no longer serve the needs of our Diaspora.

When leaders from the UJA-Federation of New York reached out to eighty Manhattan synagogues to inquire about their primary financial concerns, the overwhelming majority placed "maintenance and building-related costs at the top of their list."[2] While amounts vary, buildings of all sizes and types, in all geographic regions, require a significant proportion of a synagogue's operating budget each year—and far more when it comes to renovations or major repairs. Given their high operating costs in money, time, and energy, our sacred edifices become a purpose unto themselves, rather than the manifestation of more important missions. Moreover, they distract us from the reality that so many of our institutions lack a mission in the first place.

For many American Jews, the selling of synagogue buildings, Jewish nonprofit office space, and community centers may signal decline. However, this view loses sight of the very purpose that inspired such edifices in the first place: making a visible declaration in neighborhoods across America that Jews live loudly and proudly. As Jewish pride soars and synagogue membership falls, we see how effectively prior generations have instilled this message, even beyond the walls of buildings. As buildings deteriorate, the space for new purpose grows. With newfound time, energy, and resources, we can refocus on what lies ahead, rather than on monuments to integration into the larger society of a sort that our Diaspora achieved half a century ago.

CHAPTER 4

Power Dynamics

Too few people sit at the tables of power, and they preside over too many initiatives.

For Alex, now a Chicago-based educational professional in his midthirties, history calls him to service. The grandson of Holocaust survivors and concentration camp liberators, his family legacy is one of courage and responsibility. "Their experiences were imparted to me and embedded in me, defining my identity and place in the world," he points out. Attending a Jewish day school while he was growing up, Alex would become a leader in his teen Jewish youth group, finding his synagogue community to be the center of his life. Following the death of his grandparents and the horrors of September 11, 2001, as a teenager in New York City, Alex found even deeper appreciation for the way Judaism could help us navigate the most trying moments of life. Many of his friends, family, and clergy noticed his sense of Jewish responsibility and planted in his mind the idea of becoming a rabbi.

In the years to follow, Alex became the president of his Jewish fraternity and took on leadership roles at his campus Hillel. His nickname throughout college was "Rabbi." Following graduation, he chose to work in education to hone his pastoral and communications skills, with the principal of his school enthusiastically encouraging him to reach for the rabbinate.

Alex is exactly whom the Jewish world needs—a savvy, well-spoken, socially gifted thinker, who cares deeply about Jewish life and creatively imagined what it could become. Along with a cadre of peers and mentors, he cofounded an organization called Tribe, which redefined community for thousands of Jewishly interested young professionals in the New York area.[1]

Despite his obvious prowess as a leader, he faced rejection from the rabbinical school's admissions committee. "I was told that my Jewish experience wasn't significant enough," he recalls. "I was told that my Jewish identity wasn't developed, that somehow my Judaism wasn't what they wanted."

While sitting with a friend, sorting through this experience, Alex gained a perspective that would help define his path forward: "If you want to be a leader in the Jewish community, you can be a Jewish leader. Not every leader needs to be a rabbi." In that moment, hearing these words from the daughter of two rabbis, Alex saw that Jewish professional life was not a necessity, but one of many options. "I realized that Jewish institutions need me far more than I need them." Seldom have truer words been spoken about the relationship between a lay leader and the communities they serve. Alex is now a respected administrator at an independent elementary school. And his nickname of "Rabbi" followed him.

Alex's story also poses a challenge to us as rabbis. We, two Jewish leaders blessed to have Alex woven into our own stories, see the way in which his words and feelings challenge our own role and place in American Judaism. Alex's Jewish future will not rely on us or on people of similar place and position. It is we who now depend on finding paths of relevance and worth for Alex—and countless people like him.

In Alex, we see the emergence of a new age in which power coalesces around the people we serve and the lay leadership. Yet the Jewish community continues to invest in brick-and-mortar training programs for rabbis, cantors, educators, and nonprofit leaders, even as fewer and fewer people seem to demand them.

As of 2014, a meager 168 rabbis studied for ordination across nine institutions from the major denominations and movements in the United States.[2] The data is even more stark when Modern Orthodox seminaries are excluded. We're seeing a sharp decline in enrollment from already unsustainably low numbers, indicating that there may be fewer than seventy-five students per class year across nine campuses within progressive movements.[3] That would mean an average of approximately forty rabbinical graduates per campus (spread over five classes), with each campus requiring millions of dollars in upkeep and staffing. Tuition for many rabbinical schools hovers around $40,000 per year, and the number of students continues to decline.[4]

Why are there so many different schools? Theoretically, a single, pluralistic institution could ordain all Reform, Reconstructionist, Conservative, and Modern Orthodox students, with a lower cost structure and with more professors on the faculty. Offering a multitude of ideologies and diverse perspectives within a single institution could expand wisdom and creativity. It would be a boon for our future clergy to be exposed to an array of beliefs and practice between individuals and groups. Yet the trend in rabbinical schools has been to narrow the focus. American Jewish leaders have not cut costs and integrated seminaries, but rather built *more* of them. As Rabbis Hayim Herring and Jason Miller note:

> While it is true that Hebrew Union College, the Jewish Theological Seminary and the American Jewish University's Ziegler School have all noticed declined enrollment in the past decade, much of the reason for this is a more crowded, and therefore competitive, landscape. More options mean aspiring rabbis no longer feel compelled to matriculate in denominational-specific seminaries. The newly created liberal non-denominational rabbinical program at Hebrew College has experienced increased student enrollment in the past few years and that certainly has impacted the enrollment numbers at the more established seminaries. Yeshivat Chovevi Torah, while Orthodox, has also presented competition to JTS since it opened in the late 1990s.[5]

The focus on building new seminaries (while maintaining many long-standing ones) points to a broader trend. Why do we focus so much time and energy on a caste of professional Jewish leaders? We suggest that vested interests—namely, clergy and specialized Jewish professionals—perpetuate artificial constrictions on the marketplace for Jewish leaders, requiring them to obtain formal degrees, which take years to complete and come with hefty price tags.

The result is too few clergy and Jewish professionals to meet the demand and artificially inflated salaries.[6] Rabbis are by far the highest-paid clergy in the United States, earning 3.5 times as much as their Christian counterparts.[7] Rabbis at small to midsize synagogues earn nearly as much as "mega-church" pastors who serve communities of over two thousand people.[8] Jewish non-profit leaders can earn hundreds of thousands of dollars, with prominent figures nearing a million dollars in annual compensation.[9] Rabbinical, cantorial, and educator associations function like unions, standardizing contracts, providing salary studies that clergy can use to negotiate a raise, and ensuring generous benefits. The Internal Revenue Service allows religious nonprofits to forgo disclosing the compensation of clergy, and nondisclosure agreements are common in contracts for senior rabbis and senior cantors, creating a culture of opaqueness.

Many rabbis, cantors, and Jewish educators feel called to this path and have a passion to bring Jewish wisdom and belonging to all who seek it. But the many systems, structures, and organizations that now surround access to such wisdom and belonging can distract from this purpose and passion.

In America today, many see rabbis and cantors as a necessity for authentic Jewish experience, even though this role for clergy has been explicitly adapted from the Episcopal and Catholic churches. From baby namings to the unveiling of headstones, from the blessing of new homes to the teaching of Jewish basics, rites and rituals are grounded in a dynamic of mutual dependency. Clergy rely on the perceived value and necessity of their services and expertise, and communities rely on clergy as their conduits to the sacred. Rather than focusing clergy attention on helping individuals develop their own sense about how to practice Judaism, clergy function as gateways to Judaism and Jewish life. The typical result is clergy burnout and a communal life that is unnecessarily expensive and reliant on brick-and-mortar institutions.

While most rabbis, cantors, and educators did not enter a life of service for the compensation, that can quickly become a dominant area of interest. Rabbinical conferences are riddled with discussions of new jobs, congregational size or growth, compensation and contractual terms, and self-care for rabbis who have taken on far too many roles. Denominations define leading lights based on those with the most congregants, rather than those with the congregants who are the best served. Too few are willing to openly take risks in programming, organizational design, or engagement, because doing so entails personal risks to a clergyperson's continued remuneration.

Denominations further prioritize stability and dependability at the expense of empowerment and outreach. Prohibitions against poaching congregants from other communities inhibit competition and get in the way of consolidation of congregations.[10] These governing bodies remain focused on existing models that depend on clergy, rather than the deepening and expansion of lay leadership, which can enhance American Jewish communal life through volunteerism. Much as they may aim to support millions of congregants, they effectively centralize clergy power. The presidents of every major stream of Judaism in the United States are rabbis, reflecting publicly who retains the clout in each one.[11]

Denominational dues structures similarly hamper competition and concentrate power in the hands of clergy at the helm of major synagogues. The Reform Movement Affiliation Commitment in the Union for Reform Judaism adds a 4 percent assessment to the dues of all synagogues that belong to it.[12] As a result, a small number of large congregations provide a disproportionate percentage of the URJ's annual operating budget.[13] The clergy of these large communities—often among the most highly compensated—thereby retain a high degree of control over the denominations themselves.

The most telling example is that of the Rabbinic Visioning Initiative, which was composed of eighteen senior rabbis from the largest Reform congregations in the United States. It successfully pushed for a change of leadership within the Reform movement a decade ago[14] and, in so doing, demonstrated that just eighteen rabbis could change the course of a denominational body that serves eight hundred synagogues and well over one million American Jews.

Not only are such concentrations of power a key feature of denominations, but they also can be seen within more than a few Jewish philanthropies and initiatives in which funding has remained centered around a small number of mega-donors.

This elite echelon of philanthropists once embodied the virtues of integration in America, but their purpose did not keep up with the needs of the people whom they hoped to serve. In the words of Jay Ruderman, president of the Ruderman Family Foundation:

> When it comes to major American Jewish organizations, everyone follows the Golden Rule: Whoever has the most gold, rules. . . . You could call it checkbook Judaism—a leadership class based on wealth, maintained by millionaires and billionaires, and hardly representative of today's diverse American Jewish community.[15]

In recent decades, the two primary mechanisms of Jewish philanthropy—foundations and federations—have grown to resemble one another with donor-driven purpose and practice. As Jewish affluence grew, the leverage of such affluence in philanthropy did as well. Half of the ten wealthiest Americans are Jewish, and numerous Jewish foundations make the Forbes 200 list.[16] The result has been the elevation of large donors' interests and perspectives, even when "they run counter to those of the constituencies that Jewish foundations and federations purport to serve."[17]

They build buildings, when people need money for programs. They endow chairs at seminaries for Jewish clergy, when lay leaders need more places to learn and grow. They advocate for Israel's military might, when most American Jews advocate for meaningful steps toward peace.[18] They define Judaism genetically, when many define it emotionally, spiritually, or socially. They focus on antisemitism, while many Jews seek to understand their newfound place of acceptance and privilege.

The costs of the status quo of Jewish institutions have become far too high in time, energy, and resources. Too few people have too much influence, sit at the tables of power, and preside over too many initiatives. Clergy crowd out lay leaders. Mega-donors crowd out those who give away a higher percentage of their lower incomes. Congregations crowd out upstart communities. Denominations and legacy institutions crowd out new ways of learning and building community. We should not be surprised, therefore, that many of these mainstay institutions—and the very roles that undergird them—are in decline. Their call for their own institutional survival has become an incessant distraction from the search for higher purpose.

Yet there is another story emerging, one that shows a vibrant new American Diaspora. It is a network filled with power and potential, one growing in the cracks of declining institutions and new areas of American life. We need to create a place for Alex—and the myriad individuals who, like him, need a perch on which to stand as Jewish leaders.

PART 2

Transformations

Profound changes are afoot within the American Diaspora. The forces of affluence and antisemitism, universalism and particularism, decay and growth now collide with complex social, economic, and technological dynamics. Lay leaders are filling roles once exclusively reserved for clergy. Jews of Color, LGBTQ Jews, and people of countless backgrounds are beginning to shape the Jewish center. Israel rises as a collaborative partner, rather than a vulnerable dependent. By charting these dynamics and the intersection of the many forces at work, we begin to see a larger story of transformation.

CHAPTER 5

Blessings and Curses

Those once on the periphery of Jewish life are coming to define its center.

One of the great comedic moments from the Torah comes in *Parashat Balak*.[1] In it, the Moabite monarch Balak hires the prophet Balaam to curse the Israelites as they seek to traverse his territory. But God uses Balaam as a mouthpiece, blessing and praising the Israelites' goodness, and ultimately emerging with words that have become memorialized in the prayer Mah Tovu: "How fair are your tents, O Jacob, / Your dwellings, O Israel! / Like palm-groves that stretch out, / Like gardens beside a river, / Like aloes planted by God, / Like cedars beside the water."[2] Balaam goes on and on, bestowing blessing in place of curse.

Yet the Israelites cannot hear these words of blessing. Rather than believing they are being blessed by a foreign spiritual leader, the Israelites see threat when their men consort with foreign women. In the name of endogamy and monotheism, they slay their men. Pinchas, a direct descendant of the founding priest, Aaron, kills both an Israelite man and a Midianite woman. The humor drains from this passage as the blood pours forth. In gentler terms, one might say the same of American Jews today.

Scholars Robert Putnam and David Campbell affirm in their best-selling book *American Grace* that Americans across the spectrum of belief (and nonbelief) have a high degree of appreciation for Jews.[3] Studies conducted by the Pew Research Center in 2014, 2017, and 2019 similarly found that Jews are, on average, the most warmly regarded religious community in the United States.[4] Even though most Americans know relatively little about Judaism, they hail its growing place in the American mainstream and welcome the presence of Jewish ideas, public personalities, and even religious symbols and rituals in gentile homes and secular gathering places.

American popular culture is riddled with references to the Jewish community. From *Seinfeld* to *Shtisel*, Sarah Silverman to Gal Gadot, *Homeland* to Borat, Natalie Portman to Tiffany Haddish, Nathan Englander to Ayelet Waldman,[5] Drake to Pink,[6] Bari Weiss to Tom Friedman, to the grandchildren of three out of the last four American presidents, American Jews often take center stage in American life.

Our community has grown from 2.2 to 2.4 percent of the American population in the past decade.[7] We encounter so many conversion students that our communities cannot yet teach, mentor, and support all who seek to become Jews by Choice.[8]

Despite this numeric growth, exogamy continues to captivate our attention. It is long overdue to view it as the literal embrace of American Jews. Nathan Glazer's landmark book *We Are All Multiculturalists Now* uses intermarriage of all kinds as a measure of societal acceptance.[9] He reflects upon the extent to which our intimate lives reveal truths about underlying prejudice—and affirms that the high rate of intermarriage (which has climbed further since the publication of his book)[10] reveals most about the many who are willing to build families with Jewish people.

Intermarriage also opens up remarkable opportunities for demographic growth and social influence.[11] Seventy percent of children with at least one Jewish parent are raised Jewish, partly Jewish by religion, or with other points of connection to Jewish tradition.[12] It is anecdotally recognized among many Jewish clergy that spouses may choose Judaism long after a wedding.

It has been nearly half a century since Lydia Kukoff and Rabbi Alexander Schindler brought the concept of "choosing Judaism" to the mainstream at a biennial of the Union of American Hebrew Congregations (now the Union for Reform Judaism),[13] and with it an unprecedented rollout of programs to welcome and support conversion. For the first time since Roman antisemitism forced the early rabbis to turn inward, our institutions are reaching out and embracing the possibility of demographic growth.

The Union for Reform Judaism is now actively positioning itself for outreach to the religiously unaffiliated, with its current president, Rabbi Rick Jacobs, re-invoking the prophetic vision of becoming as "numerous as the stars of heaven."[14]

Jews by Choice now enrich countless areas of life, and popular culture provides a remarkable number of examples of conversion to Judaism. From the cult classic movie *Keeping the Faith* to the food blog *Shiksa in the Kitchen*[15] and the Unorthodox Podcast's annual "Conversion Episode,"[16] a new narrative is surfacing about Jews by Choice across cultures, genders, nationalities, ethnicities, political lines, and linguistic communities. Comedian Tiffany Haddish uncovered her Jewish heritage and affirmed her belonging in a bat mitzvah ceremony that gained international attention.[17] Ivanka Trump, daughter of former president Donald Trump, converted to Judaism within an Orthodox community.

Those once on the periphery of Jewish life are coming to define its center. Many leading lights of the American Jewish community are Jews by Choice or have affirmed the primacy of their Jewish heritage. Rabbi Angela Buchdahl reaffirmed her faith in the wake of others' questioning during her formative years and has gone on to break barriers and glass ceilings as senior rabbi of Central Synagogue in Manhattan.[18] Rabbi Sandra Lawson, the inaugural director of racial diversity, equity, and inclusion at Reconstructing Judaism, proudly asserts her identities as a queer, Black woman, a Jew by Choice, and a rabbi and has been using her growing platform to affirm and bless the multifaceted identities that more and more American Jews hold. SooJi Min-Maranda now spearheads ALEPH: Alliance for Jewish Renewal and harnesses her experience as a convert and a woman of color to create a Jewish spiritual path that is "progressive and pluralistic and non-triumphal."[19]

Top Orthodox leaders, notably Rabbi Avi Weiss, have reaffirmed a position of welcoming converts, and we are likely to see more Jews by Choice assuming leadership roles in traditional circles in the years ahead.[20] Rabbi Aaron Potek put it compellingly in his "Rabbi Rant":

> I've become much less interested in the question of whether one
> should date or marry Jewish. By focusing on the act of intermar-

riage, we ignore the far more significant questions: *What role does Judaism play in your life, and what do you want your Judaism to look like in a romantic relationship?* Though our answers may evolve over time, we don't have to wait for a relationship to address these questions. They are arguably the most important Jewish questions we will ever ask ourselves.[21]

Even some ultra-Orthodox sects are leapfrogging progressive streams by opening doors to people who might consider Judaism as a spiritual path.[22]

The Chabad Lubavitch Chasidic branch has been wildly successful at helping secular and progressive Jews feel at home in an ultra-Orthodox, traditionally gendered space.[23] Their program of *shlichut* (emissaries) reaches millions of people around the world, with over five thousand couples (a rabbi and his wife, known as a *rebbitzin*) serving thirty-five hundred institutions in over one hundred countries.[24] Chabad's operational budget is approaching $2 billion a year. A staggering 17 percent of American Jews participate in activities with Chabad.[25] These data are emblematic of the remarkable service that the organization provides, including to many who are embraced through conversion as having "Jewish souls."[26]

In building around its core purpose of *ahavat Yisrael*, the love of all Jews, Chabad strives to ignite a passion for *mitzvot* even among those most distant from tradition.[27] It centers on particular moments of ritual significance— the lighting of Shabbat or Hanukkah candles, shaking the *lulav* during Sukkot, putting on tefillin—and enables Jews to feel authentically connected, even if only for a moment, to what feels like authentic tradition.

Chabad is highly visible, not merely because of the traditional Eastern European Jewish dress that its leaders don. They seek out the public square, venturing forth in "mitzvah tanks" to areas with unaffiliated Jews, trying to show them love, care, and respect—all the while proselytizing to less traditional Jews with urgency. Chabad leaders might make LGBTQ people feel welcome but maintain belief only in heterosexual marriage; they might embrace the intermarried but see wholly Jewish households as the goal; they might give a passing nod to secular culture while claiming that such assimilationist approaches further Hitler's genocidal aims.[28]

Standing at the crossroads of a centuries-old lifestyle and modern technology, Chabad holds in tension the most trafficked Jewish website in the world, a love of all Jews, and fundamentalist views of Torah and its teachings. It is an act of bravery for Chabad to inhabit this space—much as it is for all who place the needs of others at center stage, even when doing so tests their approach to religious practice. We all experience deeply the challenges of modernity, while trying to turn its manifold opportunities into blessings.

CHAPTER 6

Prominence and Vulnerability

We owe it to ourselves and to our society to reaffirm
our potential to serve the spiritual needs of all of
those around us, even as we grapple with the fearsome
resurgence of antisemitism.

Jews comprise just over 2 percent of the American population but 6 percent of the Congress.[1] They represent 0.2 percent of the global population but 20 percent of Nobel laureates.[2] Five of the top ten wealthiest Americans are Jewish.[3] Yiddish theater was the precursor of Broadway, while Jewish entrepreneurs pioneered Hollywood moviemaking. Jewish authors fill bookstores with their works, and gentile authors contemplate Jewish characters in theirs. The residents of the White House and the Naval Observatory have Jewish family or are themselves Jewishly connected.[4] Top-tier schools teem with Jewish students, professors, administrators, and presidents.[5] Jews lead social movements and organizations across the political spectrum.

We have gone from newcomers in a land of opportunity to mainstays of American life within the span of three generations. The success of our people is staggering.[6]

At the same time, a growing number of American Jews say that they personally have faced discrimination, and the FBI calculates that nearly two-thirds of religiously motivated hate crimes target Jews or Jewish institutions.[7] American antisemitism—from the Ku Klux Klan to the Proud Boys, from the lone-wolf white supremacists who menace synagogues to the left-wing activists who cloak antisemitism in the rhetoric of the Boycott, Divestment, Sanctions movement against Israel—continues to rise. Sixty percent of American Jews report having directly experienced antisemitism in the past year.[8] The din of curses is ongoing.

In an age-old tradition, only heightened by the inherited trauma of the Holocaust, we feel compelled to circle the wagons, fight for our rights, and demand protection. And, in this time of unparalleled access, prestige, and resources, we have the means to defend our rights and beliefs as never before.

The American Israel Public Affairs Committee raises in excess of $100 million per year in its lobbying efforts and influence campaigns, to ensure that our government redoubles its strong support for and relationship with the government of Israel.[9] The Anti-Defamation League raised over $110 million in 2019 to combat anti-Jewish hate, while the American Jewish Committee garnered $60 million to engage in diplomacy on behalf of the Jewish people.[10]

Jews have also sought to secure their future and their interests through political donations. Jews contributed fully one-quarter of the total funds donated to Republican political campaigns and over half of those donated to Democratic campaigns.[11] During the 2020 election, the top fifteen Jewish donors gave more than $264 million to that year's Republican and Democratic campaigns, while fifteen of the top twenty-five political donors nationwide were Jewish or had Jewish heritage.[12]

Even excluding the myriad of smaller agencies, organizations, and philanthropies connected to security, support for the modern State of Israel, and in-reach to people who are already connected Jewishly, billions of dollars per year go to protecting the State of Israel, fighting antisemitism, and advocating for community needs.

Yet it is uncertain that this spending always fulfills a greater mission for the Jewish people. As with the story of Balaam and Balak, the present is a time of both blessings and curses—philosemitism and antisemitism, freedom to marry and freedom to leave Judaism, deep yearnings for time-tested wisdom within a society unsettled by technological change. Jewish organizations are built around the protection and integration of the marginalized immigrant community that we once were, making it possible to be both Jewish and American before we were welcome to do so in the mainstream. That mission seems increasingly outdated.

We are a "model minority" that has made stunning inroads into mainstream culture and into positions of power and influence unparalleled in Jewish history. We have become living proof that the American Dream is more than a myth. Even as we grapple with the fearsome resurgence of violent antisemitism, we must reaffirm our potential to serve a purpose beyond our own survival.

CHAPTER 7

Israel and Diaspora

The dependencies of the past are fading, eclipsed by a mutual need for relationship, growth, and creativity.

In many respects, the Babylonian Exile seeded Judaism as we know it today, evoking a process of ongoing attempts to return to a glorified past and a sacred place while simultaneously creating space and legitimacy for new practices and organizing principles. In the succeeding centuries, Diasporas in Egypt and Persia flourished, even as Jerusalem remained the Jewish spiritual center, with a Temple at its heart.

The vibrancy of diasporic traditions enabled our people to thrive when the Romans quashed successive rebellions in Judea in 70 CE and 136 CE. While the Romans desecrated the holy Temple and devastated Judean society, the great Diasporas—then stretching all the way from present-day Iran to the western edge of the Roman Empire in Spain—became the centers of Jewish life. Our early experience with dispersion safeguarded our existence for two millennia.

Communities, thinkers, and innovations all shifted toward the edges. The Babylonian Talmud, composed in what is now Iraq and Iran, became *the* Talmud and largely eclipsed the impact of its briefer and less polished counterpart created by Jewish remnants in Judea.

Our tradition remained vibrant in communities far from its geographic home. Only since the advent of modern Zionism in the latter half of the nineteenth century and the rebirth of the State of Israel in 1948 have our people been able to renew the blessings and challenges of a strong core, supported by a strong Diaspora.

In the wake of the Holocaust, countless organizations devoted themselves to building a bridge between Israel and America and then traversing it with money, people, and political support for the nascent state.[1] Israel needed the Diaspora to survive and thrive, while Israel itself provided hope for the Jewish future.

American Jews felt a new call toward Jewish unity, which became evident in both upstart Israel advocacy groups and longtime mainstays of Jewish life. So, too, did Israeli leaders work actively to bring major American Jewish organizations into the Zionist fold, cultivating their networks and learning from their political savvy. In a few short years, Zionism became a platform of American Jewish organizations, even if some American Jews remained focused on integration.[2]

With help from its American counterparts and wave upon wave of Jewish immigration from the Middle East—and, in time, many other parts of the world—Israel grew and blossomed. Even with internal tensions between Middle Eastern Jews and Eastern European Jews, an ever-stronger Israel emerged from a repeated series of crises and wars. It asserted itself as the preeminent regional power in the 1967 war and in staring down Soviet-aligned Arab states in repeated fights thereafter. All the while, American Zionist advocacy and lobbying groups continued to grow and keep Israel at the forefront of American Jewish life. Israel and American Jewish organizations complemented each other and thrived together.

By the 1990s, Israel had widespread support across a major swath of American life.[3] Not only was it a military power, but it was one that had made peace with Egypt and was moving toward peace with Jordan and the mirage of peace with the Palestinians. Israel had turned the corner from survival to self-actualization, as a place that evoked Jewish pride and universal appreciation—the embodiment of Jewish culture and civilization. So, too, relations peaked between many American Jews and their Israeli counterparts.

The unraveling of the Oslo peace process and the burst of brutality in the Second Intifada, beginning in September 2000, marked the start of a growing divide between American and Israeli Jews.[4] Many Israeli Jews saw the Second Intifada as proof that the Palestinians had never been serious about pursuing peace, having turned to violence after the Israeli government had offered them land and sovereignty. Many American Jews focused on Israel's violent crackdown on Palestinian life and its tactics of barrier and blockade building, without experiencing firsthand the wave of suicide bombings that shook Israeli society and shaped its post–Second Intifada outlook.

Israel went from being a vulnerable fledgling state to a military power in a matter of decades, and American Jews struggled to make sense of this change.[5] American Jews' traditional political home on the left called into question Israeli policy and sometimes even re-invoked old tropes about Jewish loyalty and belonging. American and Jewish aspects of identity began to grate against each other. Some American Jews took a step back from Israel advocacy but welcomed cultural and social exchanges with Israelis and Israeli organizations. Mutual enrichment rose to take the place of dependence in bridging Israel and the American Diaspora.

Since then, Birthright Israel has sent 750,000 North American Jews to Israel, helping them gain self-understanding and promoting the cultivation of their Jewish identities.[6] The Israel-based Shalom Hartman and Pardes Institutes have started American branches to bring deep Torah learning to our continent. Rabbis for Human Rights inspires activists in Israel, while its American counterpart, T'ruah, does the same in North America. United Hatzalah has brought emergency medical response times down to a matter of minutes in Israel and now does so in New Jersey, with the potential for future growth in locales across the United States.

Israeli consulates across the United States are a meeting ground for emerging and established American Jewish leaders.[7] Israeli series have become American television hits, while the American-Israel Cultural Foundation brings young talent from Israel to the Diaspora to learn and inspire.[8] Israeli bookshelves are filled with American Jewish authors, while Americans make best sellers of Israeli writers and thought leaders.[9]

Jews in the American Diaspora and Israeli Jews can increasingly engage with each other as peers. As a recent Pew study reflects:

> Jewish Americans feel a strong emotional connection with the Jewish state: A solid majority say they are either "very" or "somewhat" attached to Israel and that caring about Israel is either "essential" or "important" to what being Jewish means to them. The connection is felt both ways: Most Israeli Jews say Jewish Americans have a good impact on the way things are going in Israel. In

addition, most Israeli Jews say that a thriving diaspora is vital to the long-term survival of the Jewish people and that Jews in the two countries share a "common destiny."[10]

The emerging sense of mutual recognition between American Jews and Israel is a new dynamic, one that may shift former frameworks and require a renegotiation of the relationship. Israel stands strongly on the world stage, based on its military prowess, economic and technological innovation, and culture. Any residual dependencies now fade, eclipsed by a mutual need for relationship, growth, and creativity. Political and religious divisions present existential challenges to both Israel and the American Diaspora. A hunger for deeper learning and meaningful spiritual practice manifests with the bloom of innovative communities and educational platforms from both centers. Narratives of complex history—of racial injustice, of colonialism, and of occupation—are found within both centers. And stories of flourishing in the face of adversity, of striving toward vision and dream, blossom in both the American Diaspora and Israel.

CHAPTER 8

Sharing Power

Increasingly, spiritual power ripples out beyond the
seminary and yeshiva, in the creation of new rituals at
home, in the determination of warriors for justice, and
in spiritual guides without pedigree.

Jewish power swings like a pendulum through the arc of history between centralization and decentralization. In some eras, we see power devolve from a singular prophet to a caste of priests, to cadres of rabbis, and today to each individual. In other eras, we witness reconcentration—for example, within the monarchies of Saul, David, and Solomon—and even the self-promoting prophets who criticize it. The pendulum swings one way or the other, based on the needs of the people across time and place.

Even the biblical prologue to our history shows this trend. As slaves in Egypt, the Israelites cry out for someone else to save them. After Moses and Aaron lead them to freedom, those same Israelites spend an entire generation questioning their leaders' authority and rebelling against their leadership.

Despite his struggles leading the newly liberated Israelites, Moses focuses not on the expansion of his own power, but rather on the empowerment of the people he serves. The Book of Numbers relates the moment at which God bestows prophecy upon seventy elders, to support Moses and Aaron as they convey sacred teachings.[1] Somehow, two additional people, Eldad and Medad, begin speaking as though they were prophets. Moses's successor, Joshua, calls on Moses to stop Eldad and Medad, perhaps fearing that they will use their power unwisely. But Moses retorts, "Are you upset on my behalf? I wish that all of God's people were prophets and that God placed the divine spirit within each one."[2]

The disruption of centralized authority that so disturbed Joshua instead earned Moses's praise. Moses's dream was for ordinary people to have access to both God and prophecy without mediation by prophetic figures. That dream now defines our age.

In the American Diaspora, spiritual power does not arise from divine designation, lineage, or the fancy titles we acquire with effort. Nor is it any longer the sole province of a few spiritual authority figures. Increasingly, spiritual power ripples out beyond the seminary and yeshiva, in the creation of new rituals at home, in the determination of warriors for justice, and in spiritual guides without pedigree. In this, we see the deeper wisdom of Moses's leadership: Eldad and Medad stepped forward as prophets not because Moses asked them to, but because they themselves felt called to do so. Moses embraced, rather than opposed, what naturally emerged from his people.

Greater access to wisdom and the greater empowerment of individuals requires us to return to Moses's brand of leadership today. It means viewing the modern challenges to centralized institutions, leaders, and movements in the context of a larger vision. The American Diaspora is the strongest that Jews have ever known. We are on the cusp of a new era, defined by agency, access, and the assumption of power by more people. A movement toward individual empowerment may, in some respects, feel entirely new. In other respects, it continues the patterns we have maintained for generations, returning to the same story sparked at Sinai.

Ultimately, power increasingly resides in countless individuals, called to spiritual leadership and inspired to take on new roles in communal life. And every day in our modern Diaspora, the power of place and position diminishes. We look back and see the rise and fall of prophets, priests, kings, and rabbis. We look forward and see the empowerment of all people and the realization of Moses's vision.

This moment demands fundamental changes in Jewish institutions and the very mindset that undergirds them. We are just beginning to see new leadership and organizations rise to meet the challenge and mainstay institutions engaging in transformational change to ensure their survival and continued ability to contribute. All around, the growing impact of distributive power dynamics emerges.

Participatory philanthropy is now gaining strength, with greater power sharing and feedback from its intended beneficiaries. The recently formed Jewish Liberation Fund cites the traditional philanthropic values of distance and objectivity as "false idols" that create funding gaps and ineffective means of serving the needs of humanity. The JLF hands over its strategic direction and grant making to constituents and grassroots leaders, encouraging a diversity of perspectives and debate to ensure that relationship-building among those with different perspectives is the very structure that drives philanthropic direction.[3] Reboot and Slingshot bring together a circle of givers to help reimagine philanthropy and shape ways to inspire creative initiatives, based on the voices of millennials and members of Gen Z.[4]

Clal's Rabbis Without Borders fellowship creates cohorts of rabbis—including the authors—interested in building a new Jewish future, irrespective of denomination. Rather than reinforcing movement institutions, the fellowship forges ties around a shared desire for new ideas and ways to engage the two million people they serve.[5] Focused on rabbis (to the exclusion of cantors, educators, and lay leaders), it provides a key path for rabbis to retool and prepare for leadership in a new era of Jewish life.

Similar networks now thrive in the Institute for Jewish Spirituality, the Glean Network, Hillel's Center for Rabbinic Innovation, and the Kenissa Network. Many of these initiatives also support lay leaders in cultivating spiritual awakening, pioneering social innovation, and creating new institutions to serve the majority of Jews who lack a spiritual home. They prize collaboration over intellectual ownership and seed new ventures. They value risk-taking—both emotional and organizational—and affirm the value of collaboration as a way to maximize the chances of a venture's success. In short, they bring an entrepreneurial mindset to Jewish life.

While much of this innovation proceeds along the edges of established organizations, movements and denominations are stepping up to affirm the importance of empowering lay leadership, particularly given the financial barriers some communities face in hiring ordained rabbis and cantors. The Union for Reform Judaism's Hadrachah Seminar helps smaller congregations train laypeople in how to preside at worship and ritual experiences, so that they can lead "in support or in place of clergy."[6] The United Synagogue of Conservative Judaism's Sulam program is an intensive leadership development program, encouraging the expansion of skill sets and the deepening of leadership tools for lay leadership. In 2019, the Orthodox Union started its first lay leadership summit for women, recognizing the rising impact of women's leadership in Orthodox communities and offering a network, resources, and training tools to support their work.[7] Even as the organizing bodies of American Jewish movements seek to maintain seminaries and the traditional pathways to Jewish leadership, these new modes of lay empowerment and the expansion of leadership tracks signal this shifting center of power.

Lay leaders have similarly created new roles for themselves as spiritual leaders. The Kohenet Hebrew Priestess Institute trains women for spiritual leadership using Jewish tools and wisdom. As the institute ordains priestesses, all develop and shape their own ways of leading, often in paths quite different from those followed by traditional synagogues. Therapy, art, meditation, and energy healing are all sacred modalities through which the priestesses bring Jewish tools to meet the needs of their communities.

Hadar's Rising Song Institute is "a meeting place and incubator for creative musicians and prayer leaders who hope to reinvent the future of music as a communal Jewish spiritual practice."[8] By inspiring people of all backgrounds to engage in Jewish song and music, a rising tide of non-ordained Jewish leaders now spark new approaches to prayer and community through song around the country. ImmerseNYC started its Mikveh Guide program to train Jews of all stripes to use mikveh as a sacred ritual for many life experiences and guide others to do the same.[9]

These are but a few examples of grassroots efforts by American Jews stepping into leadership roles. It is no accident that in gatherings of Kohenet, Rising Song, and ImmerseNYC, participants are encouraged to stand in a circle. In this symbol is an acknowledgment of a leveling of power and a sense of equal access to the center. Lay leaders are reclaiming power in a way that could prove transformational for a Jewish future that relies on more participation by more people.

We are not destined to be victims of our own success as a Diaspora community. Rather, these shifting tides of power point the way to a renaissance of Jewish life. The current needs of Jewish, Jew-ish, and Jew-adjacent people already blaze new paths of belonging and engagement. By further disbursing power, we can create a community of purpose, in which every person is a creator, connector, and collaborator.

Our future lies not in mere maintenance of structures of power, but in the very changes that challenge them. As Moses witnessed new prophets emerge, he saw such new power dynamics as a measure of the success of his leadership, rather than a threat to his position. Today we see a similar pattern emerging out of the successes of past decades as a new generation of dynamic leaders rise to prominence. From Sinai to today, we have been witnessing a people called to empowerment, and today we celebrate that purpose reclaimed.

CHAPTER 9

Connecting Identities

We are asked, 'How can my story possibly fit in?'
Our answers will determine the character of our
community's future.

Without the Midianite pagan priest Jethro, the Israelites would never have survived their forty-year trek in the desert.[1] After hearing of the Exodus from Egypt, he races out to reunite with Moses. In addition to providing emotional support, he pushes Moses to delegate judicial power by appointing judges and magistrates, so that the Israelites can more readily create a just society.

This proves to be a transformational piece of wisdom. Immediately after Jethro intercedes, the Israelites gather at the foot of Mount Sinai. They can finally implement the laws that God conveys to Moses.

The notion of a pagan priest instructing Moses challenges the traditional understandings of the proper boundaries between Judaism and other faiths. So, our ancient sages began a process of erasure, implausibly casting Jethro as a convert to Judaism to simplify an identity that would otherwise raise unsettling—and important—questions about the sacred connection between Jews and people of other traditions and cultures.

It seems that Jethro had one too many identities for our sages to hold at the same time. How could Jethro love Moses and the Israelites so much that he transformed how they administered justice without being Jewish in the first place? How could an outsider have that kind of impact on the Israelites?

Sadly, the recasting of Jethro's identity mirrors the judgments and pressures that so many Jews by Choice experience today. Doing so pushes people who do not fit neatly into categories to deemphasize parts of their identity. For the sake of simplicity, many undermine the very humanity of countless people in the American Diaspora.

Given the personal nature of identity, this chapter weaves together three narratives of Jewishness and leadership alongside an analysis of Jewish identity trends of our times.

RETURN TO JEWISH ROOTS

Julia Salazar decided to run for New York State Senate in 2018. Salazar had begun to explore her Jewish roots during her time in college but did not highlight her Jewish identity during the campaign, focusing instead on the needs and backgrounds of her future constituents, few of whom were Jewish.[2] Nonetheless, in August 2018, Armin Rosen published a piece for *Tablet*, alleging that Salazar's claim of Jewish identity was a political ploy.[3] Other commentators readily joined in.

The *Forward* published an article in October 2018 titled "Why Do Politicians Keep Lying about Their Heritage?" That story compared Salazar's claims of Jewish identity to US senator Elizabeth Warren's assertions of Native American heritage.[4] The story went mainstream, with the word *controversy* repeated so many times that Julia Salazar's name was associated with it—even when few could articulate exactly what the controversy was all about or note the extent to which claims against her had come to be refuted.[5]

Julia Salazar won her seat in the New York State Senate but has not yet regained her seat in synagogue.

Salazar had first learned of her Jewish roots as a preteen, growing up in South Florida. Her father, an immigrant from Colombia, explained that the surname Salazar was Jewish and that she came from Sephardic lineage. Her father had a deep sense of faith but retained a discomfort with the Catholicism with which he had been raised. He passed away shortly before she left for college at Columbia University. Salazar feared that if she did not actively connect to her father's heritage, she might lose touch with it forever.

College gave her the chance to interact with many different kinds of Jews, including quite a few who took their practice seriously. Salazar reflects, "I wanted to explore. I had Jewish friends and was eating kosher meals with them. I started attending [prayer] services and learning basic Hebrew." She completed the conversion process, along with two other students.

Through graduation, Salazar continued to attend Columbia-Barnard Hillel and practice actively with fellow students. Afterward, however, she found it complicated to settle into a new spiritual home, which could embrace all of her identities and support her Jewish practice. She connected to Jews for Racial and Economic Justice and Jewish Voice for Peace, both of which are associated with left-wing politics and criticism of Israeli policy. She was starting to find her voice as a Jew, community organizer, and activist— but it was too multifaceted a voice for some.

The article in *Tablet* came out in the holy month of Elul, leading up to the Jewish High Holy Days. "I just wanted to vanish and allow them to win," she recalls. While some time later she began attending services with the progressive Kolot Chayeinu community in Brooklyn, she has yet to fully find her way back into Jewish community:

> The people who did this do not want me to be Jewish now. What is the point of embracing Jewish community if no one wants you to? I feel like I don't have the right to continue with Jewish learning or with *chevrutah* [study partnerships] in any Jewish way. Yet there's nothing else I could be. It's why I chose to convert. I am completely Jewish and consider my conversion irreversible.

As the American Diaspora has become integrated into the larger society and become increasingly accepted, so too has the ability of its members to define themselves on their own terms. An antisemitic society once foisted upon American Jews a unidimensional identity. But today that view is giving way to an awareness of our richer and more nuanced identities. To the outside world, a person can now fully be a Reconstructionist Jew and of Jamaican descent and Black and queer and female and Los Angelina and an attorney—and not necessarily in that order of importance. She might feel resonance with the Black Lives Matter movement at one moment, Hadassah at another, LGBTQ advocacy at a third, and congregation-based community organizing at a fourth, bringing to the fore different parts of her identity at different times.

For reasons of inertia and the residue of internalized antisemitism, many of our communal organizations continue to assume that Judaism is the only, or at least the primary, identity of those they serve and those who affiliate with them. Those who do not fit neatly into other boxes of identity may feel excluded by this assumption—notably Jews who identify as Black, Latinx, Asian, LGBTQ, immigrants, Jews by Choice, non-native speakers of English, or those of patrilineal descent.[6] As David Schraub reflects in a paper for the *Association for Jewish Studies Review*:

> "White Jews" are just "Jews"; if one is to talk about non-White Jews, a specific modifier is needed. So "White Jews" also refers to the figure of the Jew as it is currently conceptualized in the public imagination—a figure that is imposed upon the lives of all Jews, whether (individually) White or not.[7]

Today we are in an awkward, liminal space, in which antisemitism has not yet fully abated, but has abated enough that community members can reasonably demand to live Jewish lives that also affirm and even amplify their other identities. The result of the prior assumptions may be erasure not only of vibrant aspects of Jewish life, but also of a large number of Jews.

A 2019 study by Stanford University's Graduate School of Education indicates that Jewish population studies might have systematically overlooked as many as one million Jews of Color.[8] The recent 2020 Pew study on American Jews estimates that Jews of Color compose between 8 percent and 17 percent of the overall American Jewish population.[9] Some estimate that 20 percent or more of Gen-Z Jews identify as people of color, and the Pew study suggests that as many as 28 percent of Jews under age thirty identify as Hispanic, Black, Asian, or multiracial.[10]

If they're overlooked in the most impersonal of surveys, one can only imagine the pain that Jews of Color feel when entering a Jewish institution or community building, only to have their Jewish background questioned or ignored altogether. Imagine how much more alienated a Black Jew who is also LGBTQ and an immigrant must feel—even before getting to professional, political, and spiritual aspects of their humanity.

OCEAN OF JUDAISM

"How can my story possibly fit in?" For Zubeida Ullah-Eilenberg, this question reverberates throughout her life. Her father was Bangladeshi and a practicing Muslim. Her mother was Baptist and from an African American family who made their way to freedom and owned property even before the Civil War. When Ullah-Eilenberg was born, her parents chose to christen her Catholic because of the family's great affinity for President John F. Kennedy. From an early age, she conversed with God—sometimes through prayer and pleading, and at other times just by feeling the connectivity in life and the awareness of something bigger.

Ullah-Eilenberg's journey to Judaism took hold in Morocco. She found herself in a small shop looking at bracelets. As she turned to leave, the merchant stopped her, insisting she look longer and consider a purchase. The merchant called to her, "I'm not a Jew! I'm not a thief! Come back." Ullah-Eilenberg found herself shaken and fled the store, running through the old medina of the city. Two questions arose to her mind: "How does he know I'm not Jewish?" and "How do *I* know that I'm not Jewish?"

Ullah-Eilenberg would spend years studying and exploring, diving deeply into the landscape of New York City Judaism. It proved difficult to find a spiritual home, one to which she felt she could authentically bring her full self. Even after a full conversion process and an intensive adult bat mitzvah process, she still encountered a Jewish world that offered an inconsistent embrace:

> I remember one of my religious Jewish colleagues trying to lift up eugenics science, explaining that my blackness meant I was biologically different. And I was shocked. And it woke me up to these nuances about who gets to be Jewish and how even Jews with the narrative of being the perpetual outsider could still be the perpetrators of otherness.

Now, as an educator in both a Jewish day school and a congregational religious school, Ullah-Eilenberg thrives on the natural curiosity of children. She sees this curiosity as the essence of her Jewishness, for in raising questions she sees an invitation to connection:

I know who I am, and for me, my Judaism has come through endless questions—of having others question me, and me question in return. In that dialogue there is relationship, and through those questions the common thread that ties us all together gets ever more diverse and colorful. For me, being Jewish comes with the security of saying that we become wiser when we come together. And, so far, the ocean that is Judaism is always deeper than the limits set by any one person.[11]

Ullah-Eilenberg's own story illustrates the dynamism at the frontiers of Judaism as different identities and threads, textures and tastes offer an alchemy both new and ancient. We recall Moses, the infant Israelite, raised as an Egyptian, who marries a Midianite, only to then lead a mixed multitude of refugees through the wilderness. Like many of his people, he grappled with how to discern the boundaries of identity. Perhaps Moses, like Ullah-Eilenberg, exemplifies the inherent quality of a people who started as a mixed multitude. The ocean of Judaism has always been deeper than the limits set by any one person.

ULTRA-ORTHODOX ADVOCACY FOR LGBTQ JEWS

LGBTQ Jews similarly experience alienation in the face of the heteronormativity of Jewish communal life.

Born in Richmond, Virginia, Rabbi Mike Moskowitz grew up in a family with minimal connection to Judaism. Following some dating outside the Jewish community, he was connected by his mother with the Conservative-affiliated youth movement United Synagogue Youth. It ignited his interest in Judaism. But when he looked around, Moskowitz felt his true self and his environment no longer matched.

At seventeen, Moskowitz dropped out of high school to attend yeshiva. He pursued intensive studies in the two largest yeshivas in the world: Mir in Jerusalem and Beth Medrash Govoha in Lakewood, New Jersey.

For Rabbi Moskowitz, everything would change when a new question of identity came to him nearly two decades later: "Someone said to me, 'I'm not a girl, I'm a boy.' And I asked, 'But how do you know?' And this person responded, 'I just am.' And it took a few weeks of obsessively thinking about what that means until I got to the epiphany of realizing what I don't know."[12]

At the time, Rabbi Moskowitz was serving as an outreach rabbi for Aish HaTorah and Ohr Somayach at Columbia University. When he learned of Jewish day schools threatening to expel transgender students, he wrote letters of protest. He was subsequently fired, with many of his rabbis and friends severing their ties with him. Unable to serve as a rabbi in his ultra-Orthodox world, Rabbi Moskowitz was forced to take a job working in a New Jersey deli.

In 2018, during a protest in Washington, DC, Rabbi Moskowitz's words about the dignity of each and every human being struck a chord with Rabbi Sharon Kleinbaum, the leader of the largest LGBTQ synagogue in the world, Congregation Beit Simchat Torah. Rabbi Kleinbaum was so moved that she hired him on the spot. He continues to serve as the community's scholar-in-residence.

For Rabbi Moskowitz, becoming a leading rabbinic voice for trans and queer belonging did not mean an abandonment of the ultra-Orthodoxy that had rejected him. He still retains the black hat, suit, and beard customary of his community, and he continues to lead an observant life. He identifies as a cisgender, white, male, ultra-Orthodox rabbi, called to LGBTQ advocacy. At the heart of these identities, he sees Jewish wisdom and law as driving his journey: "In *halachah*, in Jewish law, we have a principle: you can't answer a question until you understand the *metziyah*, the reality . . . it's very easy to dehumanize people from a distance. Proximity is how we are challenged to see the world in new ways."

With proximity, and with exposure to new identities and realities, Rabbi Moskowitz sees growing acceptance of LGBTQ people in the most traditional Jewish circles. Rabbis and friends who once rejected Rabbi Moskowitz now refer LGBTQ individuals from their communities to him. Progressive Jews are being challenged to see ultra-Orthodoxy in a new light through his leadership, and already he is seeing more and more ultra-Orthodox families in Lakewood, New Jersey, and Monsey, New York, and around the world prioritizing proximity to their marginalized friends and family over traditional ultra-Orthodox boundaries.

The American Diaspora continues to stretch its understanding of who belongs, with growing work on inclusion of people of all racial, gender, sexual, and religious identities. Still other people call out for additional embrace: Jewish spiritual seekers, politically conservative Jews, critics of Israeli policy, and those who live Jewishly in the absence of formal conversion. While these aspects of identity are more mutable and may change over time, those who have intentionally taken them on can feel silenced as a "minority within a minority." Being a Mexican-born, LGBTQ, politically conservative Jew by Choice can leave one with few people with whom to share common ground at community events and programs, especially at a time of polarization around identity.

As awareness of, and exposure to, American Judaism's diversity grows, identities will collide and connect in new ways. Formerly separate threads will become woven together, and along with the diminishment of definition and boundary will emerge the opportunity for an even wider array of humanity to draw from the waters of Judaism. In the face of the unease we may feel from being in community with people with aspects of identity that differ from our own, perhaps we may draw from a pillar of Jewish wisdom,[13] now reinforced by modern social science: We are wisest when we're in a collective of diversity. Homogeneity dulls our wisdom, while debate and dialogue across difference encourage growth and learning.[14]

Those willing to see the opportunity of wisdom and vibrancy offered by Jews of Color, disability, multifaith families, Jewishly adjacent, and ideologies of all stripes can help nurture these new mixtures and turn Jewish communities into mosaics of creativity and belonging. Jewish institutions can become incubators of wisdom and generators of new pathways into American Judaism. The Jewish awakening has started around the periphery of organized Jewish life but will come to define the center.

CHAPTER 10

Creative Destruction

As we shed our fear of failure and communal dissolution, we can begin to enjoy the emerging bounty.

Generations after the destruction of the Temple, a group of rabbis journeyed to Jerusalem. They saw the ruins of the Temple, the former heart of the people and the house of God. They witnessed a fox scurry out from its den made in the fallen sacred stone. The rabbis began to weep for the good old days as they saw how far things had fallen. All save one. Rabbi Akiva began to laugh. They asked, "How can you possibly find delight in this?! Look at the ruin before you!" He replied, "We always knew these stones must come down. In order to move forward, this had to fall apart first. Now we can begin."[1]

We stand now before the falling stones of American Judaism. So many of the structures, boundaries, and even purposes that gave American Jews definition and texture now face seismic quakes. Rapidly declining religious participation, rising rates of intermarriage, deepening division surrounding American and Israeli politics, declining participation in Jewish philanthropy—all tell the story of decline. Widespread synagogue closures, forecast for the coming years, will challenge Jewish employment opportunities. Jewish professionals and clergy will go without work or have to retool. Jewish federations outside of major population centers will decline or fold. Seminaries should merge—though they may not, due to institutional inertia and legacy funding. Diehard Israel advocacy groups may become parochial interests of politically conservative Jews. Many Orthodox Jews will continue leaving Orthodoxy, even as higher birth rates will allow this segment of the Jewish population to continue growing.[2] Many Jews will marry gentiles or people of no religion at all.[3] The language of "continuity crisis"[4] will increasingly fall flat as coming generations become more wary of racialized frames of genetic perpetuation. The growing segment of Orthodox Jews may have less and less in common with their progressive counterparts (and vice versa).[5] Many Jews will leave the fold altogether.

The American Diaspora may be better off nonetheless.

As we gaze upon this story of decline, we recall Rabbi Akiva's wisdom. Our ancestors, reaching forward with purpose in the face of adversity, dreamed of acceptance, access, and affluence. The tenacity and ambition of prior generations built the structures and sanctuaries of our own success. But just as destruction of the Temple forced the creation of a decentralized Judaism, equipped to adapt to a world of dispersal, today we see the signs that this modern destruction also heralds a dynamic new awakening.

Institutions born of the last Jewish awakening, over a century ago, now may choose either to adapt or be left behind. Regardless, American Jews will make way for new paths to Jewish community and lives of purpose. A group that was once defined by clear boundaries of ethnicity now has permeable borders that allow Jews by Choice to reinterpret Jewish practices through the lens of another wisdom tradition—much as millions of other Americans do by embracing aspects of Buddhism (and related mindfulness practices) and Hinduism (and adaptations thereof in yoga practice). Still more will resonate with the culture, languages, food, spiritual practices, and ethical norms of Jewish tradition. Some will also see the extent to which American Jews prioritize social justice and find a spiritual home in communities that live out their values. Many with Jewish ancestry may return to a community utterly unlike the ones that their parents or grandparents rejected.

Our ancestors came to these shores largely from hostile countries in Europe. Their descendants now embody the diversity that helped America thrive, holding fast to Jewish values that encourage compassion and righteousness.

In 2020, the Pew Research Center released another major study of our Diaspora. It showed a growing Jewish population, now representing nearly 2.4 percent of the American population (up from 2.2 percent seven years earlier)—perhaps owing to methodological differences, or perhaps due to an actual growth in the self-identified population of over half a million people.[6] Nearly half of American Jews have been to Israel, many through the Birthright Israel initiative.[7] Almost 20 percent of American Jews have participated in activities with Chabad, the ultra-Orthodox outreach group, even as a significant overall majority favor clergy officiating at interfaith and same-sex marriage ceremonies.[8]

The data might feel contradictory in places, but it reveals a key phenomenon: the definition of what it means to be Jewish is changing before our eyes. Beyond the 5.8 million adult Jews (and 1.8 million children being raised Jewish "in some way"), there are 2.8 million adults of Jewish ancestry, including 200,000 of whom see themselves as both Jewish and members of another tradition.[9] Most remarkable is a third category, which the Pew Research Center describes as people of "Jewish affinity," who "lack a Jewish parent or upbringing and do not identify as Jewish by religion," but do "consider themselves Jewish in some other way." Some might well be evangelical Christians, seeking to reconnect with the Jewish roots of their tradition. But there are 1.4 million of them—equivalent to nearly one-fifth of the entire American Jewish population. When taken in tandem with 1.5 million people who are Jewish but not "Jewish by religion," it means that nearly 3 million American adults are Jewishly connected and navigating complicated, intricate questions of what it means to be so. We sense that this segment is forging new definitions of Jewish life, along with another of even greater centrality already: Jews by Choice.

While the 2020 Pew study did not focus extensively on conversions to Judaism, the 2014 "Religious Landscape Study" indicated that up to 17 percent of American Jews might be Jews by Choice.[10] If that percentage held steady or continued to rise, it would mean that there were nearly one million people who have chosen Judaism as a spiritual, social, and ethical home. Their involvements, interests, and conceptualizations of Jewish life may well constitute the future of the American Diaspora. Their lives and interests merit further study and focus in a way that the Pew study does not yet provide.

What it does provide is helpful aggregate data on Jewish self-perception. As ethnicity declines and religiosity remains secondary, more and more Jews will come to understand their tradition as one of history, ethics, and culture:

> Many American Jews prioritize cultural components of Judaism
> over religious ones. Most Jewish adults say that remembering the
> Holocaust, leading a moral and ethical life, working for justice and

equality in society, and being intellectually curious are "essential" to what it means to them to be Jewish. Far fewer say that observing Jewish law is an essential part of their Jewish identity. Indeed, more consider "having a good sense of humor" to be essential to being Jewish than consider following *halakha* (traditional Jewish law) essential (34% vs. 15%).[11]

In fact, a remarkable opportunity now presents itself. What would happen if the community focused less on a self-defeating narrative of assimilation and more on engaging the 1.4 million people with affinity and the 2.8 million with ancestry? What would happen if we listened to the million Jews by Choice and the million Jews of Color and centered them in the conversation? What if we learned what appealed to the millions seeking meaning and belonging beyond our institutions, hearing from those who might benefit from Judaism as a framework for life?

Therein lies the path to renaissance, and therein lies an awakening taking shape right before us, with human needs coming before institutional norms. By transforming such need into purpose, we can renew our Diaspora.

It is worthy of rabbinic parable: There was once a lone Jew wandering the roads of Babylonia. In the midst of his wandering, he witnessed two birds engaged in fierce combat. The victorious bird then plucked leaves from a small plant and applied it to the foe he had killed. Miraculously, the bird stirred and came back to life.

After witnessing this miracle, the man said, "I shall go, and I will revive Israel." He went to the plant, took a bundle of its leaves, and set out with this new purpose. Along the way, he encountered the carcass of a fox. When the man touched the plant to the fox's body, the fox came back to life and ran off. The man then came upon a wounded lion and applied the magic plant. The lion's wounds healed and the lion was revived. The lion then rose, roared, and devoured the man who had saved its life.[12]

In the eyes of the early rabbis who wrote this tale, this is the story of the Jewish people. The wanderer carries a sprig of life on his travels toward the Promised Land—even when doing so subjects him to peril.

We as a people carry a myth born of very real trauma—the sense that the history of the Jewish people is simply a string of persecutions and near exterminations. From Philistines to Romans, from Crusaders to Inquisitors, from Stalins to Hitlers, we often mark the progression of time by tragedy and horror.

But, of course, if this were the only story, it would end with the demise of Judaism, the lions of history forever consuming the naive and foolish traveler. Our history—and surely the rhetorical implication of Babylonian rabbis writing this parable—tells another tale, that there is another layer to this narrative. There is another story of the Jews.

This is a story of the wandering life-giver. It is the narrative of a people who could bring produce and infrastructure to Egypt, law and ethics to Europe, philosophy and trade to Spain; the history of a people who could innovate industries of finance and trade; the tale of a people filled with Arendts, Spinozas, Einsteins. A people who could take a barren desert land and transform it into a country of technological, agricultural, and cultural renown. A people who could take adversity and scarcity and harness them into opportunity.

We possess a history of traveling the world, reaching toward vitality and vibrancy in every age. A story beyond survival. A story of continual revival.

This story ripples with optimism. It names the lions of adversity and yet articulates a source of renewal. Even in the cycles of vitality and decline, creation and collapse, there is an arc of movement toward a mythic Promised Land. Through different eras and geographies, this tension-filled story elevates Jewish purpose wherever our wanderings take us in Diaspora. It suggests that our greatest challenge may also afford us new opportunities for revitalization. Today, this story cycles again in the great American Diaspora.

As the Jewishly inspired move away from legacy institutions, such institutions will become increasingly out of step. The inspired, more nimble organizations will retool, and new ones will rise. We are already witnessing the early stages of this process of renewal.

Remarkable people are coming to the fore to meet this moment and could come to define the norms of American Jewish life in the future. Some work in institutional mainstays, rededicating themselves to movement building, while many more are creating their own networks and places of belonging in structures yet to become the norm. Still more are reclaiming ancient practices or repurposing existing ones in service of the underserved and spiritually disenfranchised. Economist Joseph Schumpeter's notion of a "gale of creative destruction"[13] is blowing through Jewish life, uprooting and transforming everything in its wake. After we lose the ever-present fear of failure and communal dissolution, we might give ourselves permission to enjoy the emerging bounty. In this case, the bounty derives from people and their creativity, which we endeavor to chronicle in the sections ahead.

PART 3

Renewing

This new awakening is bursting forth in response to unmet human needs. Nearly every facet of American Jewish life faces disruption—and the prospects for renewal. In every corner of our community, Jewish identity, wisdom, ritual, and power are being remixed and reimagined. As centralized authority declines, American Judaism moves and grows in a multitude of directions. As technology reduces the importance of geographic boundaries, new opportunities for connection and new modes of exercising power emerge. New mixtures of ancient Jewish practice and modern needs are beginning to shape the renewal of American Judaism, widening access to Jewish wisdom and ritual, transforming Jewish consumers into Jewish co-creators, and building new networks of Jewish belonging.

CHAPTER 11

Spiritual Renewal

Early innovators of open-source spiritual practices were people left off the biggest bimahs and the traditional centers of communal power.

In the Book of Samuel, when Hannah prays at the temple in Shiloh, a priest so mistakes her silent supplications that he assumes she is drunk.[1] Hannah was deviating so significantly from the norms of animal sacrifices that he could not fathom any other explanation. In so doing, Hannah exemplifies how radical departures in ritual can become central to Jewish tradition if they answer a deep spiritual need, even as they may have been profoundly misunderstood at the outset. Thousands of years later, "prayers of the heart" and words that arise from the depths of our being remain integral parts of Jewish prayer.[2]

The rituals of the American Diaspora have evolved, steadily and inexorably, since its inception. Much of what today we consider mainstream is the remnant of earlier spiritual breakthroughs. Jewish immigrants from Germany and Eastern Europe swelled the ranks of American Jews, moving melodies and traditions away from their Sephardic counterparts who had arrived when America was still a Dutch colony. They then sought to establish new American Jewish rituals, as we see with Rabbi Isaac Mayer Wise's audaciously titled *Minhag America* (American rite) prayer book from 1857.[3] By 1894, the ascendant Reform movement had created its first *Union Prayer Book*.[4]

In the ensuing race to establish ritual norms for the swelling Jewish population, we see still more transformations. Ascendant American denominations sought to differentiate themselves through the presence of organ music in synagogues—or prohibiting it.[5] In 1922, Rabbi Mordecai

Kaplan officiated at the first bat mitzvah service, for his daughter, Judith, generations before the ceremony became a mainstay of Jewish life.[6]

We are living through another period of rapid innovation in the norms of ritual as we adapt to a time of social and technological change. While some of these changes will remain outside the mainstream, others are becoming increasingly central to the American Diaspora. From the feminist reclamations of mikveh with Mayyim Hayyim and ImmerseNYC to Hadar's Rising Song Institute; from Ritualwell's soulful life-cycle ceremonies to the spirited approach to communal prayer of Jewish Emergent Network communities and millennial- and Gen-Z-driven pop-ups and prayer minyans; from the reclamation of Jewish renaming rituals (*shinui hashem*) following a harrowing experience or illness to the reimagination of such ritual to give a sacred frame to transgender affirmation; from the Jewish Renewal movement's adaptation of other faith practices to the Institute for Jewish Spirituality's retreats and online meditation opportunities, the American Diaspora is experimenting with and reinventing the very core of Jewish ritual.

OPEN-SOURCE RITUAL

In her award-winning book *Inventing Jewish Ritual*, Professor Vanessa Ochs describes the process of rethinking ritual: "Rather than blaming Jewish tradition for its being hard to penetrate or complaining that synagogues are boring and cold places, you can take responsibility for your own spiritual well-being by shaping Jewish experiences that resonate with your world and your life."[7] Dr. Ochs suggests that this empowered reframing started well before widespread use of the internet, with the release of *The Jewish Catalog* in 1973 by Richard Siegel and Sharon and Michael Strassfeld.[8]

The book, which spawned second and third editions through 1980,[9] documented the wide range of evolving Jewish ritual and created opportunities for Jewish connection to a far larger group of potential ritual leaders and practitioners:

> You did not have to be ordained or even "religious" to practice or design and introduce new rituals. You did not have to resolve any theological issues: you could ritualize whether you were sure, unsure, or undecided about God's presence. You did not have to be

a member of a congregation or a denomination. If you were seeking company, with the catalog's "blueprints for a *havurah*,"[10] you could create your own alternative antiestablishment, antiauthoritarian community for study, celebration, fellowship, and activism.[11]

The Jewish Catalog helped people experiment openly with tradition and celebrate an enormous breadth of ritual possibilities.

Jonathan Sarna indicates that *The Jewish Catalog* also brought the grassroots prayer groups of the *havurah* movement to the mainstream, with book sales that set records for its Jewish publisher.[12] It provided an accessible source of Jewish tools for those on a spiritual journey:

> The widespread return to ritual that soon became evident across the spectrum of American Jewish life, the renewed interest throughout the community in neglected forms of Jewish music and art, the awakening of record numbers of Jews to the wellsprings of their tradition—these and other manifestations of Jewish religious revival in America all received significant impetus from *The Jewish Catalog*.[13]

The *havurah* movement has echoes today within Moishe House, which expanded from a single communal living experience and now supports Jewish communal living in twenty-seven countries and reaches seventy thousand people per year with its programs.[14] As its founding CEO, David Cygielman, reflects, "We don't have to be on the cutting edge, because we let our young leaders take the lead" and focus on helping them create "memories, immersive experiences, meaningful relationships, and connections to Jewish clergy."[15]

Another successor of *The Jewish Catalog* is the open-source platform for ritual innovation Ritualwell. In an effort "to make contemporary feminist Jewish liturgy and rituals broadly accessible," Kolot: The Center for Jewish Women's and Gender Studies at the Reconstructionist Rabbinical College and Ma'yan: The Jewish Women's Project, a program of the JCC in Manhattan, cosponsored the website in 2001.[16]

Today, Ritualwell's 350 contributors have created over sixteen hundred new rituals, and more than 250,000 people access it each year.[17] Its cofounders, Dr. Lori Hope Lefkovitz and Rabbi Rona Shapiro, created a platform to connect people seeking Jewish inspiration and meaning with innovative rituals for countless moments in life. With curation and quality control, Ritualwell now directly connects seekers with immersive learning experiences and mentoring from accredited clergy.[18] It demonstrates how rituals live beyond the walls of the synagogue and are driven by human needs. And it illustrates a way in which ancient ritual may spark modern innovation when leaders make Jewish tools accessible on an open-source platform.

Professor Ochs highlights the connection between marginalized people within organized Jewish life and the creation of new rituals.[19] These rituals derive from the need to live fully and Jewishly beyond the constraints of traditional liturgy while still engaging in dialogue with it. Today, this need continues to drive ritual innovation regarding gender transition and LGBTQ affirmation, the embrace of Jews by Choice, the blessing of Jews of Color, and the recognition of people who are not Jewish but are entwined in Jewish life. With the internet making accessible Jewish texts, ideas, and rituals, we are entering an era in which rituals are not something defined by elite religious leaders, but rather are marked by open access and empowerment of more people than ever before.

SACRED SONG AND SUMMER CAMP

While *The Jewish Catalog* may indeed be seen as a move toward far greater engagement and a key step toward open-source ritual and community, there was a second force that laid the groundwork for ritual empowerment: Jewish summer camps for youth.

Dating back to the 1890s, Jewish summer camps provided respite for America's Eastern European newcomers and the chance to leave urban areas and continue the process of acculturation within a safe context.[20] Camps were seen as eminently effective in enabling new immigrants to integrate both their Jewish and their American identities. The camps were so successful that their numbers ballooned from one hundred to almost thirty-five hundred during the twenty-three-year period starting in 1910.[21]

By the 1940s, mainstream denominations and institutions began recognizing the potential of Jewish summer camps.[22] For increasingly secularized

Jews, they became a laboratory for ritual and a model of the ideal Jewish community.[23]

Camps provided another, unexpected opportunity for the development of new ritual—song, with new melodies, verses spanning languages and ideologies, and emotional cadences elevating the voices and spirits of campers and counselors alike. By the 1920s and 1930s, a special time was set aside for the camp "sing-along," and the song leader was elevated to a formal role.[24] By the 1950s, singing became central to Jewish camps, and by the 1960s, individual camps began creating repertoires of their own.[25] Their melodies joined in harmony with those of Jewish folk singers, from Arlo Guthrie to Peter Yarrow and Simon and Garfunkel.[26]

Song leading became a new path to leadership, first within the Reform movement and, in time, within other movements of Judaism.[27] It came to define the youth group experience and ultimately transformed synagogues from within. From the Jewish camp experience emerged musical forces that transformed Jewish liturgy, prayer, and practice. Notable among them was the voice of Debbie Friedman, who became a musical pioneer and also began to weave together the "song session" with formal Jewish prayer, expanding musical leadership beyond the clergy.

Friedman's 1972 debut album, *Sing unto God*, built on her formative years in the Olin-Sang-Ruby Union Institute, a Reform camp in Wisconsin, and provided a new set of songs for Shabbat, which went well beyond traditional liturgy and encouraged widespread participation in sacred music. Friedman later reflected, "My own experiences and the spirit of the Institute came together to allow me to create in the finest educational and spiritual moment of my life. That is when I knew that *Sing unto God* was only a beginning."[28]

Over the course of twenty albums, innumerable concerts, feminist gatherings, and song sessions, Debbie Friedman transformed the way Jews across denominations pray. Much as some Reform synagogues might play a melody by the Orthodox rabbi Shlomo Carlebach[29] for Shabbat, so too might an ultra-Orthodox Chabad House sing a version of *havdalah* by the Reform-trained Friedman. For all the ways in which sharing of ritual or understanding of text may be complicated across different streams of Judaism, music often transcends ideological bounds. It brings people together in song and invites more people into spiritual leadership—far beyond the archetypical older male synagogue cantor. It provides a new vision for Jewish sacred music: participatory, mellifluous, and empowering of disenfranchised groups—including women and LGBTQ people.[30]

For twenty-five years, the gatherings of Hava Nashira, "the official Jewish worship and music conference of the Reform movement,"[31] have trained, supported, and inspired song leaders.[32] Grounded in so much of Debbie Friedman's creative work, Hava Nashira at the Olin-Sang-Ruby Union Institute searches for future innovators in sacred music, Jewish song, and ritual renewal. It gathers hundreds of budding musical talents for four days each year for the chance to collaborate, workshop, learn, and build what is next.[33]

Musician Joey Weisenberg has launched the even more intensive Rising Song Institute within the pluralistic Hadar Institute[34] to support Jewish musical leadership across denominations and walks of life.[35] It has become a gathering place for leading Jewish vocalists and instrumentalists, with a fellowship and musical residency to support artists, an ensemble of "master musicians," master classes, and a platform for individuals to deepen their awareness of Jewish music and support communities that "join together regularly to study nigunim [wordless melodies], nusach [prayerful melodies], and Jewish musical wisdom."[36] Recent collaborations between the Rising Song Institute and the National Museum of American Jewish History have garnered over ten thousand views online.[37]

TRANSLATING TORAH

Spiritual innovators are disrupting even the most central rituals of synagogue life. Long before he was ordained a rabbi or deemed a "maverick,"[38] Amichai Lau-Lavie found himself in the role of teacher and "translator."[39] In 1999, while teaching Torah at Congregation B'nai Jeshurun on Manhattan's Upper West Side, he began to experiment with theatrical interpretations during the Torah service. He found this new role to be a way of, in his words, "challenging the patriarchal, misogynistic" nature of the text, and he "experimented with the notion of turning the Torah service into a live performance."

What began as an experiment "snowballed into a theater company and a nonprofit"—and ultimately a "method" and cohort of practitioners. One question led to another: "We sort of became a community and became interested in adapting Torah and the Torah service. But this was just the first step. What happens to theology? What happens to theology if we translate that?"

It expanded to Yom Kippur services, then Rosh Hashanah services, and then the question of a spiritual community: "In 2008–2009, we took a year to figure out how we could do this more regularly." He was striving to create "equal footing of the written and the spoken, the ancient and the contemporary." Once ordained, Rabbi Lau-Lavie could be a "rabbi to artists" and not just an "artist to rabbis." His congregation, Lab/Shul, lives on as a center of ritual generativity and theatrical community. The congregation draws on sacred text, bringing ancient ideas into modern dialogue and drama called Storahtelling. Storahtelling continues to be at the heart of innovations in *b'nei mitzvah* ceremonies, trainings for "clergy, educators, and artists,"[40] and services dedicated to the translation of sacred text into contemporary, theatrical terms.

Much as Rabbi Lau-Lavie used theater to translate Torah, Sara Lefton, as she put it, "sparks connections to Judaism through digital storytelling," with creative, engaging, and musical cartoons of each Torah portion, other sacred texts, holidays, and rituals in her educational nonprofit, BimBam.[41] She reflected in an interview with the Bernstein Family Foundation:

> Coming from a small Southern city where there wasn't a lot of this available, and since I was working online, I thought—I can create web-based Jewish learning! Essentially my idea was to create a Schoolhouse Rock for Jewish learning, and I kept thinking—I cannot rest until this thing exists! So here I am now.[42]

As a parent herself, Lefton attributes her success to the way in which animation can open children's minds and eyes to Torah learning and Jewish life: "Everyone knows that it's so transformative. Especially anyone who's a parent. Saturday morning cartoons are like magic."[43] It was a way to connect that was genuinely fun and did not require parents to be experts in Jewish life. BimBam's viewership mushroomed, branching out into content for adults, teaching resources, Judaism 101,[44] and the complete rethinking of Jewish educational standards and pedagogical approaches.[45]

While BimBam has wound down its independent operations, its videos live on as part of ReformJudaism.org and remain a source of inspiration across denominations, age groups, formal communities, and countless people who span the spectrum of Jewish connections. By the time of its acquisition, its 450 videos[46] had been watched eleven million times on YouTube,[47] with syndication across many Jewish publications and platforms, and likely reached a multiple of that number in classrooms and other group learning settings. With resources that endure in their significance, BimBam's impact will continue long after the sunsetting of the nonprofit organization that launched it.

JEWISH SPIRITUALITY

Rabbi Rachel Cowan was a Jew by Choice and a pathbreaking leader in making Jewish spiritual practices accessible to fellow clergy and laypeople. In 1990, she became part of a quintet of female leaders who founded the Jewish healing movement, which took Jewish practice and wove Jewish ritual into spaces of illness, infertility, and mental health.[48] All five leaders faced serious illness—their own or that of loved ones—and had not been able to find Jewish rituals, communal supports, or places of reflection adequate to their needs. Rather than lamenting the absence, they joined forces with Rabbi Amy Eilberg to establish a network of what became forty Jewish healing centers across the country.[49]

Rabbi Cowan reflected with quintessential humility on the groundbreaking work: "We knew that relationships and community were the key to healing. So, we devised healing services, wrote prayers for patients and doctors alike, created mikveh [a ritual bath] rituals, and ran support groups. We helped revitalize synagogue *bikkur holim* [programs for visiting the sick] groups."[50]

From the Jewish healing movement, Rabbi Cowan went on to develop Jewish spiritual resources for countless moments in life, changing the way a generation of Jewish leaders understood spirituality and, in time, empowering countless other Jewish people to access it as well. She cofounded the Institute for Jewish Spirituality (IJS) with Rabbi Nancy Flam and a cadre of Jewish thought leaders.[51] They did so in response to the observation that many Buddhist teachers and students in the United States had seemingly Jewish names, yet seemed not to find the contemplative spiritual practices they sought within the Jewish tradition of their roots.[52]

Following Rabbi Flam's tenure as founding executive director, Rabbi Cowan took the helm of IJS from 2004 to 2011 and brought it from the fringes of Jewish life to the center.[53] It has since trained Jewish leaders and renewed the influence of traditional spiritual practices within Jewish communal life.[54] IJS has brought resources and classes online and sparked new interest in Jewish spiritual practice and learning among laypeople across the country.[55]

At nearly the same time as the Institute for Jewish Spirituality was taking root, Dr. Alan Morinis, Rabbi Yechiel Yitzchok Perr, and Shoshana Perr cofounded the Mussar Institute to make the nineteenth-century spiritual practices of Rabbi Israel Salanter accessible to a wider audience.[56] Rabbi Salanter's teachings suggested that for each of us, every moment can be filled with holiness if we make enough time to reflect and make intentional, righteous choices. The Mussar Institute continues to flourish and bring reflective Jewish practices to people of all ages and across organizations.[57] It elevates laypeople and gives them the tools to lead lives of purpose. It is part of a wave of online platforms, books, resources, and courses of practice and study.

Ritual renewal ripples from new centers of community life. Today, the leading lights of Jewish sacred music need not be cantors, while rabbis need not be involved in rituals at all. The Jewishly inspired are rising to break spiritual monopolies and assume greater agency in their spiritual experiences. Groups of leaders emerge organically—or are seeded by clergy who recognize that spiritual leadership is an exercise in empowering others.

CHAPTER 12

Reclaimed Practices

Today our trajectory is one of decentralization,
empowerment, the creation of new paths to holiness—
and the reconsecration of long-standing paths in
which we have found new meaning.

Throughout Jewish history, dispersal has preceded revival and innovation. Following the exile from Eden and the terror of the biblical flood, humanity rebuilds. The construction of Babel, a citadel reaching toward the heavens, serves to unite humanity with shared purpose. So successful is this building project that God cautions, "If, as one people with one language for all, this is how they have begun to act, then nothing that they may propose to do will be out of their reach."[1] And so God scatters humanity and diversifies language.

Commentators through the millennia have attempted to discern the message of this tale. At times, it is read as a warning against human hubris; at other times, an affirmation of people's potency or as a remonstrance against homogeneity. But it is clear from the biblical text that the blossoming of difference is meant to be read as a divine course correction.

Throughout Jewish history, this dispersal from Babel would serve as a narrative anchor for future dispersals. With the rise of Babylonia as a center of Diaspora Judaism, rabbinic theology would draw from the trope of the Tower, bringing God into Babylonia and from there out into the diverse corners of the globe and history.[2]

God is a presence found in each moment of disruption and fragmentation. The early rabbis imagine God's presence in the stability of the Temple and also in dispersal into synagogues and study halls. Today our trajectory is one of decentralization, empowerment, the creation of new paths to holiness—and the reconsecration of long-standing ones in which we have found new meaning. In an effort to illustrate these new paths, we focus on three examples: the reclaiming of the mikveh, the Passover seder, and the ethical will. These span both personal and communal domains, illuminating these trends of decentralization and empowerment through the reimagining of ancient practice.

MIKVEH

The mikveh, or ritual bath, was once seen as an artifact of Orthodoxy and its patriarchal notions of family purity.[3] It was used primarily after a woman's menstrual period and before she resumed sexual relations with her husband.[4] Nearly all of the 365 Jewish ritual baths in the United States were Orthodox—until twenty-five years ago, when progressive streams of Judaism began to reclaim the practice.[5]

The first Reform mikveh was built in 1995 by Temple Israel, in West Bloomfield, Michigan. In 1999, Shir Ami Bucks County Jewish Congregation in Newtown, Pennsylvania, completed its own mikveh. Then in 2000, Anita Diamant wrote a transformational essay, titled "Why I Want a Mikveh." She saw the potential to reclaim mikveh for embodied practice, community, feminism, and pluralism. Her vision would serve as the backbone of Mayyim Hayyim, a nondenominational mikveh and education center that opened its doors near Boston in 2004. In its first few years, it hosted more than forty-five hundred immersions, and in June 2006, Mayyim Hayyim held a national conference to encourage networking and sharing of best practices regarding mikveh.[6] By 2019, Mayyim Hayyim celebrated its twenty thousandth immersion and three thousandth conversion to Judaism and helped seed and support the building of inclusive mikvehs in more than two dozen locations.[7]

Beyond inspiring renewed interest in embodied Jewish spiritual practices for people of all genders, denominations, and expressions of Jewish life, Mayyim Hayyim also renewed paths to spiritual leadership for laypeople. It trains entire cohorts to be mikveh guides—facilitators of sacred ritual, educators about mikveh, and pastoral counselors—to use immersion as a way of supporting people experiencing infertility, pregnancy loss, relationship ruptures, and coming-of-age rites.

Following a transformational personal experience of mikveh at Mayyim Hayyim prior to her own wedding, Rabbi Sara Luria decided to intern there while in rabbinical school. Following her ordination, Rabbi Luria founded ImmerseNYC in Manhattan to further expand access to mikveh as a ritual for all, as well as furthering the work of lay empowerment as mikveh guides.[8] After training hundreds of guides, who in turn helped support thousands of immersions, in 2018 ImmerseNYC was brought under the umbrella of the Marlene Meyerson JCC Manhattan, the first community center to offer mikveh education.[9]

In 2018, Mayyim Hayyim, ImmerseNYC, and numerous other inclusive mikveh organizations collaborated to create the Rising Tide Open Waters Mikveh Network. By weaving together dozens of mikvehs and communities pursuing mikveh, Rising Tide helps with shared resources, trainings, and leadership. Through their annual retreat, Rising Tide brings together the energies of inclusive *mikvaot* to amplify their work and further expand the network of mikveh guides and ritual resources throughout the country.

SEDER

Matzah—the bread of affliction—gives us a taste of slavery. But must it always taste quite so bland? An entrepreneurial power couple do not think so.

Abounding with hipster snark and spiritual calling, Mitzvah Matzos is a countercultural twist on this mainstay of Passover food. Founders Naomi Baine and Rabbi Barry Dolinger sought to make matzah that actually tasted good and was not driven by a need for shelf-stabilization in the mass-produced crackers that frequent seder tables.[10] Mitzvah Matzos is now a registered nonprofit that raises awareness about the forty million slaves in the modern world and fights human trafficking.[11]

Dolinger believes that process is as important as product and that in reconnecting with the process of creating matzah, we can reconnect with Passover—its meaning and its lessons:

> The Passover story is about liberation—liberation from systems of oppression—and so the rituals surrounding it give us the opportunity
> . . . to see Jewish behaviors as inspiring societal change. That's what
> we are seeking to do through matzah. We are literally trying to make

the experience thicker and denser, just like the matzah we make. We take dozens of volunteers, we source local wheat harvested and milled without slave labor, we donate the proceeds to support causes that end human trafficking. We harness authentic Jewish ritual to change perspective and systems.[12]

As one of the most celebrated holidays, Passover inspires families across the world to create immersive sensory experiences. We light candles to mark the start of the holiday. We sing familiar songs. We drink four cups of wine. We taste the matzah. We encourage participation by having the youngest children ask four questions. We retell the story of Passover in an annual symposium on freedom.

And how we do so has also become the subject of great renewal and discussion. Author and teacher Mark Gerson affirms the central place of the Haggadah as a vehicle through which we share the story of our people's liberation:

> We tell the story of the Exodus, therefore, through a book that essentially curates the Greatest Hits of Jewish Thought with sources long before and after the great event itself. This alone constitutes a radical interpretation of the Exodus. Constructing it this way, the authors of the Haggadah were saying that the Exodus was not an event that began and ended but one that previous Jewish experience was spent preparing for and all subsequent Jewish experience is still living.[13]

The "guidebook" of the seder is the Haggadah, and its reconstitution each year is becoming a ritual unto itself. While prior generations relied on Maxwell House's classic Haggadah or one of the many other mainstream guides, the process is now one of co-creation, customization, and radical reinterpretation of the guidebook and corresponding rituals.[14]

Continuing with innovation surrounding the celebration of Passover, Haggadot.com has transformed the way in which people co-create and customize Jewish ritual guides. Its user base has ballooned to the point that it has become a central design lab for Jewish rituals throughout the year. These rituals, in turn, inspire hundreds of thousands of people[15] and empower tens of thousands to become authors of their own traditions:

Haggadot.com is a design lab for the Jewish community, experimenting with technology, media and user experience to imagine new formats for engaging in ancient traditions. Our platforms, Haggadot.com and Custom and Craft, enable over 100,000 users annually to make their own haggadahs and other DIY materials for Jewish ritual. We facilitate new product development through collaborations with leading Jewish organizations and thinkers across a diverse spectrum of perspectives.[16]

Haggadot.com empowers coauthors and ritual leaders of all backgrounds to own their religious experiences. It encourages Jewish organizations to become "core content partners and makers,"[17] by elevating their approaches to ritual onto a global platform, while also giving access and ritual-creation tools to all its users. Its how-to guides train people to lead seders of all kinds, while blessing the wide spectrum of forms that such a seder can take.

This sense of empowerment and the process of co-creating and customizing Haggadot and other ritual guides has become a significant draw. A staggering 450,000 people visited Haggadot.com in 2020, with 86,000 downloading one or more Haggadot.[18] Eliminating social and financial barriers transforms the practice of the Passover seder. Haggagot.com's success is archetypical of a platform that connects thought leaders, artists, and practitioners and points to the future of ritual creation as a sacred Jewish practice.

ETHICAL WILLS

While serving as director of volunteers at the Hebrew Home of Greater Washington, Hedy Peyser cofounded what became Lessons of a Lifetime: The Ethical Will Project.[19] Descended from a prominent Eastern European rabbi, Isaiah ben Avraham HaLevi Horowitz, Peyser knew of his ethical will as a document that transmitted wisdom from one generation to the next. Some scholars traced the ethical will's origins to the Torah, suggesting that the first ethical will came in the form of Jacob's frank reflections to his children at the end of his life. Traditionally, these documents were for great people. Could they be revived as a more universal practice to gather and transmit the wisdom that each individual had to share?

Peyser concluded that most people did not record an ethical testament because of the emotional and logistical labor required to do so and because they were afraid they lacked the requisite wisdom. They needed a format and a set of questions to prompt their reflections and insights.

What began as a foray into the wisdom of seniors soon involved the volunteers as well, most of whom were in their teens or twenties. In an increasingly formalized training process, Peyser encouraged young volunteers to record each other's ethical wills, noting that people of all ages have much to teach.

Dozens of young volunteers and older adults were connecting, talking about life's most important moments. The seniors were grateful for what Peyser termed "a willing ear," while the younger participants felt a renewed sense of purpose and access to the wisdom of another generation.

The program expanded to sites around the Washington, DC, area and, more than a decade after its founding, still helps other organizations adapt ethical wills for their members. A document as ancient as the Torah has been revived for the benefit of countless individuals, of all backgrounds and ages.

CHAPTER 13

Connecting from Afar

While in-person gatherings retain great power, hybrid rituals that include an online component are here to stay, so that people can connect wherever they are and be part of important life-cycle moments, even if from afar.

Amid the darkest days of the Covid-19 pandemic, Jonah Bleicher and Min Ding welcomed their daughter Freda Moon Ding into the Jewish people. Jonah is originally from Israel, while Min is originally from China and converted to Judaism in the United States. Both are filmmakers, with family members and friends spanning the globe.

With only Min's mother present in person, they brought circles of loved ones together across three continents for a ceremony with two rabbis—one in New York, one in Jerusalem—and in four languages—English, Hebrew, French, and Chinese. Together, they bestowed words of blessing upon baby Freda and felt the closeness of relationship, even while thousands of miles apart.

The pioneer in spiritual technology was Jonah's mother, who had been using the pandemic to explore synagogues around Israel, picking and choosing among the programs that she liked the most. It was her idea to involve her rabbi in Jerusalem, Haim Shalom, along with Min and Jonah's rabbi in New York.

Min noted that it was "more meaningful than other Jewish rituals" that she has been a part of, "even though without technology it would not have been possible." She reflected that the extensive preparations heightened the experience of seeing people from China, France, Israel, and around the world.

An enduring concern, even among those who elect to hold them, is that rituals conducted online might feel ersatz and emotionally disconnected.

Yet a surprising number of rituals appear adaptable. The *beit din* (a rabbinic court, which, among other things, interviews potential converts to Judaism) has welcomed people into the fold, while Introduction to Judaism classes now take place online with students who span the globe.

Sophia Cohen converted to Judaism during the Covid-19 pandemic, following a year of study and far longer contemplating her family's Jewish roots.[1] She found a way to create a hybrid ceremony, with a *beit din* online with her sponsoring clergy and a mikveh experience in the ocean. She emerged from her private experience in the ocean with a sense of "rebirth" and then joined with her family and closest friends to celebrate this transformation. In person and online merged into a continuous whole of experience, affirming Cohen's place within the Jewish people. She suspects that hybrid ceremonies will become more common, especially given the comfort that many digital natives have with online experiences.

Min, Jonah, Freda, and Sophia are but some of the countless people who have connected to prayer and life-cycle ritual as never before, using technologies to span distances great and small. Baby namings, *b'nei mitzvah*, funerals, and shiva minyans all now take place online, with ever-evolving formats and customs.

While in-person rituals retain their power, multi-access rituals that include an online component are here to stay, so that people can connect wherever they are and be part of important life-cycle moments, even if from afar. This will, in turn, promote conversations about accessibility, convenience, informality, and the sacred nature of time and space in Jewish traditions. It may also challenge notions of Jewish community.

The Rabbinical Assembly of the Conservative movement adopted a resolution that enables them to reach people online, which Reform and Reconstructionist communities had already been doing.[2] The result was the unwinding of geographic monopolies and a profusion of "shul shopping," based on content, leadership, and fit, rather than physical proximity. Many distant synagogues instantly became reachable and attractive, by virtue of the fact that people could connect from their homes and there was no physical space open for them to go.

Kol Nidrei services at Central Synagogue in Manhattan drew 34,000 views on YouTube, 22,000 on Facebook, and tens of thousands more via livestream and the Jewish Broadcasting Service in 2021.[3] Yom Kippur morning garnered even more views, with 40,000 on YouTube and 28,000 on Facebook—not counting thousands more for the family services, lecture, and contemplative music, nor the livestream or JBS broadcasts.

IKAR in Los Angeles drew nearly eight thousand people to its streaming of Yom Kippur services on Facebook in 2021, while Cantor Azi Schwartz's melodies have "gone viral" from the *bimah* of Park Avenue Synagogue since long before the pandemic, with more than a million views on some of his videos of traditional prayer conveyed through novel melodies.

Even weekly Shabbat services have seen a significant rise at communities across the country, as the pandemic made options available to them free, and free of any social anxiety associated with entering the physical building of a religious institution.[4] Since reopening their physical spaces, many synagogues continue to draw far larger numbers of participants online.[5]

The pandemic pushed us beyond the threshold of geography and allowed people to feel present from afar. This recent leap in our understanding of spiritual community and belonging is part of a larger trend of change. Technology and the pandemic are allowing for new responses to fundamentally human needs for ritual, connection to a shared past,[6] and a sense of continuity amid a time of uncertainty. The larger story is one of empowerment, personalization, and innovation within Jewish rituals themselves. It is about total inclusivity, the welcoming of people irrespective of background, identity, or how they engage Jewishly. It is highly individualized but also connected to a greater whole, and it bridges distance through a sense of shared time.

Residents of Munich may soon join Chicago congregations in order to pursue adult education opportunities. Tuning into beautiful Friday evening services streamed from Michigan or Texas can evoke a sense of belonging. Some do not miss the *oneg* snacks and conversation or *kiddush* luncheon after services, while others have found effective ways to re-create these in online breakout rooms. Place can shape prayer, and so can medium. In turn, computers are coming to shape community, rendering a "community without walls"[7] increasingly viable for learners, pray-ers, and advocates for Jewish causes.

The declining significance of geography may likewise hasten a reorganization around niche and focused purposes. Some communities might become the best centers of Jewish baking, while others will redouble their focus on Jewish mindfulness; still others will become centers for Jewish outreach and conversion;[8] and still more will turn into places for successful people or those aspiring to success to network or learn about Jewish ethics in the workplace.

CHAPTER 14

Praying with Our Feet

A growing number of justice organizations reside between the traditional centers and the growing periphery of the American Diaspora.

A growing number of organizations are forming with the explicit purpose of mediating between traditional centers of American Judaism and the growing social and economic justice needs of the American Diaspora. They seek to influence the center and to train traditional leaders to better serve those whose ranks are growing but still feel as though they are on the fringes of Judaism. Their models are innovative and inspired to do good in an effective way, often looking to make systemic change well beyond the boundaries of the Jewish community.

Rabbi David Saperstein, the director emeritus of the Religious Action Center of Reform Judaism and former US ambassador for religious freedom, dedicated his career to establishing social justice as a center of American Jewish life. Working with Reform leaders Al Vorspan[1] and Maurice Eisendrath,[2] he galvanized social action committees in synagogues across the country and across denominations. The synagogues, in turn, came up with new ideas, which this cadre of justice-minded leaders at the center could cull and share as best practices. From mitzvah projects done by *b'nei mitzvah* to Mitzvah Day to hunger awareness programs during the High Holy Days, the Religious Action Center created an extraordinary network of individuals, groups, and communities that kept justice at the center of their existence.

In many respects, these efforts have succeeded. In assessing the qualities that American Jews believe to be important to their own Jewish identity, 47 percent chose "a commitment to social equality," compared to 24 percent who picked "religious observance" and 13 percent who selected "support for Israel."[3] New movements are afoot to bring this energy to the center of mainstream American Judaism, harnessing the power of networks dedicated to the common good.

Two social justice organizations that illustrate well these new approaches are Jews for Racial and Economic Justice (JFREJ) and IfNotNow (INN). Both are known as gathering places for Jewish progressives who feel less than welcome in other organizations. Over time, they have each created a sense of belonging for people who might otherwise not have a communal space in which to express their Jewish identities.[4]

Audrey Sasson, executive director of JFREJ, reflects on the opportunity that her organization has to effect change:

> We have a responsibility to engage as many Jews as possible in this work. We have a congregation of people who join and pay dues. People buy into the vision of the organization and find their place in it. We work to build a strong Jewish left.
>
> It's more polarizing right now to say that the Jewish left has a mandate to organize alongside others. [Yet] there is a role for Jews to organize in progressive coalition.[5]

JFREJ utilizes a community organizing approach, focusing on building personal relationships and activating them in target campaigns. Based in New York and founded three decades ago, it stresses economic justice and anti-racism. With a clear sense of mission, JFREJ can forgo much top-down oversight and train activists to carry on its work directly.

IfNotNow has similarly thrived by giving voice to Jews whose primary identity resides within progressive causes and politics. Morriah Kaplan, director of political education and training for IfNotNow, suggests that the mushrooming organization built upon "a lot of existing networks and organizing," notably alumni from the Habonim camps (which draw upon roots in Labor Zionism), J Street U, and the Jewish Organizing Institute and Network in Boston.[6] Alumni of these groups felt as though every couple of years there was another war in the Middle East, and they wanted to prepare for the next one and affirm that, as a reflection of Jewish values, they cared about the well-being of Palestinians.

Kaplan suggests that INN has created a "big tent anti-Occupation group" for people who span the spectrum from anti-Zionists to passionate Zionists, all of whom believe that the Israeli government needs to end its presence in the West Bank and take more seriously the humanitarian needs of Palestinians. It gained traction in its public responses to the 2014 war in Gaza.

IfNotNow's leaders initially tried a diffuse organizing structure, sending local leaders a "movement in a box," with core tenets of the organization and strategies for creating an affiliate. That approach flopped. INN's organizers realized that they needed more structure and support from professional staff.

Kaplan became a volunteer trainer and, more recently, joined INN as a full-time member of its staff. The intensive trainings were condensed into two days, from nine in the morning until six in the evening, with four or five different modules each day, led by two trainers with a team of fifteen to twenty people. INN staff would then step in to provide support after the training. They often found that the retreat was participants' first meaningful Jewish experience.

The election of Donald Trump as president in 2016 proved to be another galvanizing moment: "In the three or four months after the election, we trained five hundred people. That's when we expanded the staff from three to eight." In the years since, INN has refocused on a team to equip and train new affiliates and keep them connected to the national organization.

Kaplan lists its achievements: "We've reached [nearly] five thousand people who have come to workshops and panels. Our email list is forty-two thousand, and our best-performing videos reach tens of thousands—or a million or two for our very best ones." INN's members give in time at least as much as they give in financial resources, enabling the organization to continue growing with a minimal annual budget of approximately $600,000.[7]

Like JFREJ, INN launched a political lobbying arm, which actively endorsed candidates in the 2020 elections and sought to get them to take positions on the Israeli presence in the West Bank and US aid to Israel. It plans to continue gaining in visibility through political actions, which complement its organizing and community-building work.

By directing Jewish activism toward policy in Israel and against traditional Jewish centers of Zionism, INN and JFREJ enable progressive American Jews who stood beyond the margins to feel a sense of belonging and purpose. One can actively oppose human rights violations in Israel and be a proud Jew and even a passionate Zionist, bringing a new formulation of American Jewish identity into focus and giving organizations structure to create community and have an impact.

Another formulation of Jewish activism is developing to serve Jews who identify as both politically progressive and proudly Zionist. Eighty-two percent of American Jews say caring about Israel is either "essential" or "important" to what being Jewish means to them. Half of American Jews define themselves as politically liberal.[8] Yet in an American political landscape that increasingly aligns liberalism with anti-Zionism, many Jews feel a painful tension between aspects of their identity.

In 2017, the Chicago SlutWalk, an annual protest against rape culture and police violence, banned Stars of David and Israeli flags from their march. That move concretized the growing sense that Israel affiliation and perhaps even Jewish affiliation are contrary to progressive politics.[9] This led Amanda Berman to gather friends and peers to demonstrate and challenge this image of banning Zionism from progressive activism. She ultimately founded the organization Zioness:

> Zioness is a place to go where we do not have to cede this space of progressivism. Social justice is in our veins, and we shouldn't have to bash Israel for credibility. We need to confront the binary that being a Zionist means that we oppose Palestinian rights or liberation.[10]

Two years later, the Dyke March in Washington, DC, barred Jewish pride flags from being displayed out of concern that they were symbols of Zionism and therefore antithetical to the principles of inclusion for the march.[11] This proved to be a pivotal moment, and the Zioness movement spread rapidly across the country, with more than thirty chapters to date.[12]

Each geographically based chapter brings focus to local issues, encouraging supporters to reflect upon how their Jewishness and Zionism inspire and reinforce their social justice activism. In Chicago, the focus is on reproductive justice; in Raleigh-Durham, advocates work on ratifying the Equal Rights Amendment. Experimenting with community-organizing methods, Zioness is another quickly expanding movement, offering new space for American Jews to be politically progressive and proudly Zionist.

JFREJ, INN, and Zioness all merit our attention for the way in which they bring together justice and advocacy for Jewish causes, mainstay institutions, and community-organizing initiatives, all within a social start-up. They rean-imate the long-standing tradition of American Jewish participation in social movements and the belief that we are stronger when we stand in solidarity with others but do not lose our unique voices.

CHAPTER 15

Studying as Sacred Practice

New platforms and online content aggregators can curate offerings for the growing audience of Jewish learners, who need not leave their living rooms to participate in conversations that transcend identities, borders, and ideologies.

Rabbi Leon Morris, president of the Pardes Institute of Jewish Studies, believes that the American Diaspora over-invested in prayer spaces and under-invested in houses of study. He suggests that the house of study, the *beit midrash*, is sorely missing from the American Jewish landscape and could be a path to renewal for a community filled with open discourse, keen minds, and spiritual skepticism.[1] The Pardes Institute is drawing upon its alumni, many of whom were or have become key Jewish leaders, to engage more laypeople in communities across the country. It has piloted some intensive courses of study and is seeking to use technology to link in-person and online efforts in Jerusalem and across the United States.

Rabbi Justus Baird, senior vice president of the Shalom Hartman Institute's North American branch, reflects on the renewed focus of learning in the Diaspora. The Shalom Hartman Institute used to have only a fundraising arm in the United States but came to realize that its programs could bring meaning to American, Canadian, and Mexican Jews. It seeks to give rabbis and other Jewish leaders an infusion of great Jewish ideas. Like Pardes, the Shalom Hartman Institute is trans-denominational, egalitarian, and hoping to inspire communal renewal through new ideas. The institute contends that the current period of spiritual renewal in the State of Israel is best defined in terms beyond a stand against antisemitism.

Perhaps the most established center of intensive, pluralistic Jewish study in the American Diaspora is Hadar, whose mission has long extended beyond Jewish professionals and lay leaders to empower "Jews to create and sustain vibrant, practicing, egalitarian communities" of Torah, prayer, and loving relationships.[2] Rabbi Elie Kaunfer, one of Hadar's cofounders, reflected that "we started Hadar twenty years ago with a prayer experience . . . and we saw that what was needed with Jewish prayer ended up being what was needed for Jewish learning as well."[3] Sensing this growing need for connection to classical text, Hadar created a relationship-based mode of study:

> The educational arm of our work was born out of this belief that if you let the power of Jewish wisdom shine forth, people would be drawn in and connect to it at a much deeper level. It's the content of what is taught, the way or purpose with which it is taught, and then the relational connection between people that is often what emerges when you study the content.
>
> For a long time, Jewish wisdom has been communicated through some relational connections. That is a key aspect we really felt was underplayed in the American Jewish scene. In essence, that is Hadar—believing in the power of the content and believing that building relationships around study would both open up the content and also open up people.[4]

Since its first eight-week summer course in 2007 for just eighteen students, Hadar's enrollment has ballooned, with classes and events reaching tens of thousands of people each year. Alumni are also empowered to create their own initiatives, which now reach countless more learners.[5] Its online Project Zug program brings together two thousand people annually in online study partnerships, and its resources for prayer and study have been downloaded over three million times annually worldwide.[6]

Like Rabbi Morris, Rabbi Kaunfer ultimately envisions study as key to the future of Jewish identity. He sees Hadar at the leading edge of a fundamental change in what it means to be Jewish—to learn, to acknowledge our intellectual limits, and to create deep relationships that help us gain self-understanding and awareness of the world:

For me, I imagine this being the ultimate redefinition of "Jewish." That one day we could say, "Oh, you're Jewish? That means you study ancient texts with deep wisdom and expansive questions with another person." For me, that would be an incredible sense of twenty-first-century Jewishness and an amazing world in which to live.[7]

A similar ethos pervades Limmud North America, which found inspiration in the Limmud conferences and learning events that are a hallmark of Jewish life in the United Kingdom. David Singer, executive director of Limmud North America, says that their efforts are grounded in "the firm belief that the strength of the Jewish people is built through relationships, not organizations" and that "learning is the most powerful way of connecting people," particularly in a Diaspora in which people "flourish across silos."[8] Singer criticizes the mentality of fear that pervades many Diaspora institutions: "We are so afraid of decline that we don't invest in the creative thinkers of today."

Limmud actively works to fill the gap, empowering "independent communities of grassroots leaders" to build "local Limmud organizations," which comprise "a movement engaging tens of thousands of people in Jewish learning" and "empowering Jewish journeys." It "begins with the premise that every person has value to add in building Jewish community" and that "every person can be a student, and every student can be a teacher."

The local organizations, now found in eighteen North American communities,[9] focus on immersive learning experiences, festivals with renowned speakers (who typically are not clergy), a day of study honoring the *sh'mitah* year of agricultural rest in Israel, the counting of the seven weeks between Passover and Shavuot in brief daily gleanings via email,[10] and programs driven by the 150 lay leaders and 1,000 volunteers who serve as conveners at the local level.[11]

According to Singer, "Limmud is more interested in empowering people to curate Limmud experiences than to partake in those experiences." In "bringing in new classes of leadership to build Jewish experiences," it "transforms communities" in ways that can be "replicated across the continent" with "grassroots [mobilization] like none other in the Jewish world." Ultimately, Limmud seeks to effectuate systemic change and refocus

Jewish communities on the wisdom of each person and the fundamentally Jewish process of learning, discourse, and personal growth.

STUDYING ONLINE

For many Jewish organizations, even as Jewish learning typically conjures up the image of bustling study halls, conference rooms, and lecture halls, more and more seekers of Jewish knowledge are finding new paths to wisdom in nontraditional, nonphysical spaces. The media organization My Jewish Learning views technology as a key piece of reaching, teaching, and inspiring Jews across the country and around the world.

According to Sharon Weiss-Greenberg, the former director of education partnerships at My Jewish Learning, the website welcomes one million visitors each month, with thirty thousand receiving daily Daf Yomi emails (about the page of Talmud that some study each day until completion of the entire series in seven and a half years), seventy people attending the daily Kaddish minyan (prayer service), and live events averaging two hundred to five hundred people in attendance.[12] Its intensive programs have a far larger footprint than the largest synagogues in the United States and may transform the way that entire swaths of the Jewish population view Jewish study.

Spurred on by the pandemic, My Jewish Learning recently positioned itself as the warehouse for Jewish ideas and programs online, launching a subsidiary website called the Hub. A year after its pilot, twenty-three thousand people receive its daily events email,[13] while countless more participate in ongoing programs, curated in an easy-to-access and easy-to-search listing of events.

The initial pilot launched with half the content created in-house and the rest created by partner organizations. Subsequent iterations of the Hub have been much more partner-focused, giving people easy access to first-rate content from synagogues, learning centers, and Jewish institutions across the United States and well beyond.

In addition to bringing together disparate organizations—250 as of August 2021—the Hub created a space for experimentation and learning about what was working (or not) in online Jewish learning for adults. Site organizers are systematically studying what learning programs and content gain traction and attendance.

Weiss-Greenberg emphasizes the importance of spotlighting and studying best practices, challenges, and new interpersonal dynamics that have become evident on the Hub and in so much of communal life online: "Organizations that have never heard of each other could work together. Instead of working in silos, we can work together."

My Jewish Learning is part of an archipelago of websites dedicated to Jewish content, from Kveller, on Jewish parenting; to Alma (heyalma.com), on Jewish feminism; to the Jewish Telegraphic Agency (JTA), on news from around the world and how it affects Jews. My Jewish Learning exemplifies how disparate journalists, bloggers, and social entrepreneurs can amplify messages (through cross-posting), generate revenue (through online advertising), and motivate a growing base of readers and thought leaders. It now uses its data-gathering capabilities across platforms to even better serve people hungry for Jewish ideas and current events. In time, it could expand further into the space of spirituality and worship and come to compete directly with existing religious communities in a way that would spur still more innovation.

My Jewish Learning regularly cross-posts and references content from an online platform recently hailed as "the greatest Jewish website in the world,"[14] Sefaria. As one of its stalwart funders affirms, "Sefaria's founders . . . envisioned a world in which any interested person could have unfettered access to the entire Jewish canon."[15] What once were inaccessible or even arcane texts are now freely searchable, frequently translated, and compiled with three million intentional linkages between texts, commentaries, and more recent thinkers.[16] Its boosters boast that Sefaria was organizing the "entire core Hebrew canon" of Jewish texts, spanning continents and centuries.[17]

Jewish clergy lean heavily upon Sefaria for adult education sessions and sermons. Yet its greatest impact has been the democratization of sacred wisdom. With thoughtful translations and an open-source process of translating and linking texts, Sefaria lifts thousands of texts out of the yeshiva and Judaic library and makes them accessible to the public.[18] Users can create and share study guides for particular areas of interest; these are searchable by the wider community. By 2019, Sefaria had created two hundred thousand of them.[19] These guides, in turn, empower more people to become teachers of Torah,[20] preachers of Torah, and learners who return day in and day out to thoughtful reflection about the texts and ideas that define our people. By 2020, more than half a million people used the Sefaria platform to support their studies each month.[21] What once required fluency in Aramaic and years of formal tutelage is now accessible and engaging to anyone with a computer, an open mind, and spiritual yearnings.

WOMEN'S INTELLECTUAL LEADERSHIP

Much as with innovation in sacred music and spiritual practices, groups marginalized within the American Diaspora have brought study toward the center of American Jewish life. These include a remarkable number of Jewish women.

In Rosh Chodesh study groups, women mark the new month of the Hebrew calendar and reflect on the nature of menstruation, reproduction, and embodied Jewish experience. At feminist Passover seders, they give voice to the prophet Miriam and the midwives Shifra and Puah, as well as countless other female leaders whose roles were diminished in biblical and rabbinic text and the retelling we do each year at our seder by reading the Haggadah. They are "standing again at Sinai,"[22] writing feminist Torah commentaries,[23] and even breaking glass ceilings as equal participants in Orthodox yeshivas.

Rabba[24] Sara Hurwitz founded Yeshivat Maharat in 2009 to ordain women as Orthodox clergy.[25] Within a dozen years, it had ordained forty-nine clergy, with forty-five more in the course of their studies.[26] Rabba Hurwitz reflected on becoming the head of a yeshiva: "My heart and my soul felt the most comfortable, and I wanted to create that opportunity not only for myself, but for others."[27] She noted impatience with and frustration over the lack of women's voices in Orthodox feminist circles and even in talking about women's leadership. At its core, study at Maharat is intended to empower women to serve the Jewish people and nourish their spirits in the process.

In the course of the seminary's admissions process, Rabba Hurwitz finds a way to ask every prospective student, "Do you love the Jewish people? Do you love Torah learning? And do you love God?" If you do, "and you have a deep desire to take those loves and share them out [in] the world," Yeshivat Maharat is "the right place to nourish that."

Rabba Hurwitz likens Yeshivat Maharat to "sort of an emerging teen" in "a really great place of stability and growth." It has grown more than she could have possibly imagined back when she started with three students who had uncertain job prospects following ordination: "We have sixty women who are going through our programs," and many are finding jobs and pathways to leadership within Orthodox communities.

Even as new leaders embark on formal training as clergy, countless others have found paths to study as laypeople, and new institutions have arisen or established American branches to meet the need. The Shalom Hartman Institute, the Pardes Institute, and the Hadar Institute are leaders in this emergent sector. That two of the three are based in Jerusalem shows the extent to which study can also foster intellectual and social exchanges between Israel and the Diaspora.

Dr. Judith Rosenbaum, chief executive officer of the Jewish Women's Archive (JWA), leads a model organization focusing on learning online:

> History is a study of change over time. So if you're interested in change, you have to be interested in history. I believe we are helping people understand themselves as historical agents. And if you are a historical agent, part of what you're doing is making an impact and trying to make change in the world today.
>
> When we were founded, the "Archive" part of our name was controversial, because we weren't a traditional kind of archive—we don't have a physical collection, we were digital only, in the very early days of the internet. We were redefining what an archive was, reimagining it for the twenty-first century, and creating access to history in new ways. Our goal, in part, was to democratize history by making it accessible to anyone, from anywhere.[28]

Dr. Rosenbaum sees the archive as a digital space that enables people to see how their story dovetails with the wider Jewish story. She notes:

> I think a lot of people who are trying to understand where they fit in the Jewish story feel like they can come through JWA in a different way than they could through a mainstream Jewish institution, like a synagogue, where they're going to show up with a sense that there's an agenda or there are expectations. Our goal is to expand the Jewish

narrative, so that more people see themselves represented. It's very exciting to me that, thanks to JWA, people all over the world, from all different kinds of backgrounds, are now encountering Jewish history, many for the first time, through the stories and experiences of Jewish women. That was never possible before. We start with the issue of gender, but we don't stop there. Any reassessment of the narrative opens up the question: What else have we left out? Who else haven't we been looking at? What other stories haven't been told? We've added women back into the story, and we've thought about [other issues as well]: Have we also ignored class? Sexual orientation? How have we ignored race? Geography and ethnic Jewish identity?

New platforms and online content aggregators can curate offerings for the growing audience of participatory Jewish learners. Thanks to technology, these Jewish learners need not leave their living rooms to partake in conversations that transcend identities, borders, and ideologies.

PART 4

The Unfolding
Awakening

In this new awakening now taking shape, we can see the potency of collective action unfolding all around us. In the chapters ahead, we map numerous ways in which others are stepping into the challenges of the times and the many new possibilities they are offering our community. We see a move away from passive pleas of survival and toward dynamic modes of becoming and belonging. The very forces that are upending our formerly stable world are also presenting a path toward our promising future.

CHAPTER 16

Reaching

Our community has begun reaching Jews where they are socially, emotionally, and spiritually, rather than demanding the conformity required for protection during times of great external hostility.

Our community once faced inward, surrounded by a wider society that rejected or even tormented Jews. As widespread antisemitism faded in twentieth-century America, so did notions of a simple binary between American and Jewish identity. Our community has begun reaching Jews where they are socially, emotionally, and spiritually, rather than demanding a degree of conformity necessary for protection in a time of great external hostility. Those once deemed on the margins of Jewish life are finding meaningful ways to connect, albeit often outside of traditional institutions. Many of the initiatives that reach them are free of cost or subsidized for participants, which provides a risk-free way to explore Jewish life. They answer a core human challenge—loneliness—which they address through new visions of community found on a digital platform or as a loose network.

LONELINESS

OneTable uses Shabbat dinner as a way of responding to the essential human need for connection. Its core concept is that people—especially young professionals from the millennial generation and Gen Z—are facing loneliness and burnout and could build their personal communities by enjoying a much-needed pause around the Shabbat dinner table.[1] It uses a digital platform to match hosts and guests and offers ideas and resources for thematic dinners and gatherings, as well as funds to subsidize the cost of hosting. For highly mobile young professionals and graduate students, that can mean uplift, tradition, and the path to more regular social contact. It also enables One-Table to glean data about the needs and desires of rising generations of Jews—uncovering the reality that, for most participants, celebrating Shabbat is a key motivator.[2] By October 2017, it had brought together fifty-five thousand people for nearly two Shabbat dinners apiece.[3]

Even as it touts other metrics of success, Birthright Israel might have succeeded most at bringing emerging adults into community, into relationship with one another, and into relationship with Israel. It has paid for more than 750,000 young Jewish adults and young adults with Jewish ancestry to participate in a ten-day tour of Israel. It is of a scale like few other outreach initiatives in the history of our Diaspora—or any Diaspora. While it is touted for increasing the rate at which Jews marry other Jews,[4] even more importantly, it provides an immersive Jewish experience for an entire generation, and perhaps more to come.[5] Birthright is linked to measurable increases in the number of Jewish friends, holiday observances, attendance at communal events and religious services, and a feeling of connection to Israel.[6] It engages Israel as a living laboratory of Jewish life and helps young adults find community and friendships that endure long after the trip is done.

An offshoot of Birthright Israel is Honeymoon Israel, which focuses on intermarried couples and uses a subsidized trip to Israel for the newly married as a path to Jewish community and identity. Cofounded in 2013, it responds programmatically to the Pew Research Center's *A Portrait of Jewish Americans*,[7] which notes that 58 percent of American Jews who are not Orthodox marry someone who is not Jewish.[8] Rather than telling people whom to marry, the program builds a sense of community through shared experience and the blessing of a deeply Jewish wedding gift. Venturing to Israel in groups of twenty couples, with a guide and the presence of a local rabbi, the participants are 26 percent more likely to feel connected to Jewish life after the trip[9] and have a peer group with whom to explore Jewish life going forward, as well as a clergy point of contact for experiences connected to communal life. While the program is far smaller than its Birthright counterpart, its attentiveness to and affirmation of intermarried couples and its thoughtful path to community-building and Jewish exploration provide an updated and helpful frame for engagement. By acknowledging that even the most loving of couples can feel isolated when they do not have a clear community on which to call and friends with whom to experience life's joyful moments, Honeymoon Israel welcomes these intermarried couples into the Jewish fold.

COMMUNITY AS NETWORK

PJ Library was founded in 2005 as a program to send Jewishly themed children's books free of charge to families in western Massachusetts.[10] It was intended to be a path to greater Jewish connection for families with young children. According to Meredith Lewis, the longtime former director of content, education, and family experience at PJ Library, they initially anticipated a total of seventy eligible subscribers with Jewish homes or connections to Jewish family—but found seven hundred people who wanted to sign up: "These people didn't want to be on a listserv. They wanted to be connected to Jewish values and ideas." In focusing on the home and all the people in it, irrespective of Jewish background or prior institutional connection, PJ Library created a pathway to Jewish learning, greater communal involvement, spiritual inquiry, identity formation, and networks of peers working to navigate Jewish parenting.

The initiative has grown rapidly, both across North America and around the world. According to Lewis, by 2021 it had more than 680,000 subscribers receiving books monthly, in more than thirty countries and in seven languages. It has local partners in places around the world, both to ensure that books can remain free of charge and to supplement the reading with community programs and opportunities for social connection.

PJ Library has discovered Jewishly connected families that other institutions had not been able to identify. In many locales, 110 percent of anticipated eligible Jewish participants sign up, looking for ways to connect Jewishly that might not currently exist. For established institutions, it provides a way to reach institutionally unaffiliated Jews and pique their interest in Jewish life.

Going forward, PJ Library plans to focus on titles representing the many different kinds of Jewish families and ways of being Jewish. Lewis asserts that "seeing yourselves in the stories matters. We have not yet exhausted all of the stories; there are so many that we haven't told. . . . Our core product has not seen anywhere near the end of its life cycle."

It is not only children who need to be affirmed and engaged Jewishly. So, too, do people at other important milestone events and formative life stages. The organization 18Doors helps interfaith couples and families access meaningful Jewish professionals and resources for life-cycle rituals. It has never been a brick-and-mortar organization, but an online gathering place for people seeking Jewish connection, officiation, and learning—without judgment or fear of criticism. With a large majority of American Jews marrying people of another tradition or background (58 percent and rising as of 2013),[11] 18Doors provides free online resources, points of contact in local communities, and a list of clergy who are eager to preside at weddings, baby namings, and other rituals for couples in which one spouse is not Jewish. At present, these officiants perform ceremonies for seventeen hundred to two thousand interfaith couples per year.[12]

Jodi Bromberg, chief executive officer of 18Doors, affirms, "We have two core audiences—new interfaith couples and [interfaith] parents of young children, ages zero to six. Our website has a lot of resources and stories from other couples—resources on Jewish values, life cycle, and a Jewish clergy officiation service."

Unlike most communal organizations, 18Doors has been entirely online from its inception in 1998.[13] There was no need for an expensive physical plant or staff infrastructure, so the growing platform and community could remain nimble. Bromberg reflects that "at that point, there wasn't a place for interfaith families to go for support." The goal was for interfaith families to "hear other stories from families like theirs, in a supportive way" that could lead to Jewish involvement.

Since then, it has branched out, working with entire metropolitan areas to hold in-person programs and provide a pathway to community for interfaith families. Yet such community-wide initiatives were resource intensive, and many locales were unable to sustain the costs. The leadership of 18Doors came to recognize that it could more efficiently help existing clergy retool and refocus their efforts on outreach to interfaith families than build an entire programmatic structure from the ground up. It has established a two-year Rukin Rabbinic Fellowship to train, support, empower, and provide resources for cohorts of fifteen to twenty rabbis across denominations, who host programs, share ideas, and study problems that interfaith couples face during their interactions with 18Doors or their clergy officiants.

Bromberg has also taken note of PJ Library's successes in building a core service into a resource for Jewish professionals and the communities they serve:

> This year we're launching a program lab to take advantage of the rabbis' creativity, meshed with the types of topics that interfaith couples often come to us about. These then feed into a program bank, which has an additive program component—in the same way that the PJ Library had a creative program bank for the engagement of professionals on the ground. It's not just about one rabbi and one community, but the potential to offer similar programs in other communities, using that program bank and resources.

Both 18Doors and PJ Library are looking beyond typical notions of community to digital platforms, networks, customer discovery through free niche services, and data-driven approaches to problem-solving. They are looking beyond typical notions of Jewish couples and families to welcome in those who might otherwise languish along the periphery. Their gleanings, and the gleanings of those who follow suit, will come to guide future communal institutions—and upend the outdated status quo.

CHAPTER 17

Being

Our institutions remain outdated in their notions of belonging, wasting precious energy on questions such as whether Jewish clergy should bless an interfaith wedding, rather than actively embracing people who seek Jewish learning and spiritual practices.

C lement Price, public historian of the city of Newark, New Jersey, and professor of history at Rutgers University, reflected that "race is a social construct."[1] He explained that Ashkenazic Jews, Italian Americans, Irish Americans, and countless other groups used to be seen as nonwhite and only became perceived as white within the past generation or two in the United States. If these notions of race can change based on external perception,[2] can other aspects of identity change over time based on internal perceptions of self? Increasingly, that seems to be the case.

Over the past half century, formerly fixed understandings of identity, such as gender and sexuality, have become increasingly fluid. Each person's dimensions of being are filled with tension, nuance, and intention, presenting both a challenge and an opportunity to the notion of Jewish identity as well.

Transgender people might take brave steps to live in the embodied form that feels right to them. A growing number of people experience different expressions of gender at different times. Still others feel a fluidity in their sexuality.

If something once thought to be as immutable as gender and sexuality can increasingly be seen as an ever-changing continuum, so, too, can religion. It is no longer a contradiction in terms to think that a person can have a deeply Jewish experience in one moment and a deeply Buddhist experience in the next—or, for that matter, a sense of Jewish culture and ethnicity, coupled with Buddhist spirituality and practice.[3]

Even the notion that one is exclusively part of the Jewish people as an ethnic group no longer works, if it ever did. It is not a contradiction in terms to be Native American and Jewish, Hispanic and Jewish, Black and Jewish, Asian and Jewish. One can eat Chinese food on Christmas both because of the Jewish American tradition of doing so and because one was born in China, before moving to the United States for work and to Israel for an MBA.[4]

What has become evident in the past decades in the United States is that people are embracing ever more intricate and multifaceted identities, which emphasize some parts more than others at different times or prove fluid altogether. While Jewish denominations used to thrive in the United States because they provided a menu of options for a consistent and predictable customer type, they are declining in strength, number, and outright relevance as the dimensions of identity vary more and more in our increasingly multifaceted Diaspora. Manifestations of gender, ethnic, spiritual, and political identities can be mutually reinforcing at some times, while at other times they might create friction. Sometimes one area of identity might be more prominent, while at other times a different facet of identity might come to the fore.

The Ashkenazic, heteronormative, nuclear-family-centered, static assumptions of Jewish communal life may inadvertently hurt people who don't fit neatly into those categories when they seek to engage with communities and organizations whose implicit assumptions exclude them. As a result, they may feel marginalized. Many of our institutions remain outdated in their notions of belonging, wasting precious energy on questions such as whether Jewish clergy should bless an interfaith wedding, rather than actively embracing people who seek Jewish learning and spiritual practices.

Author and journalist Susan Katz Miller powerfully describes her disaffection with many Jewish communities who do not embrace interfaith families:

When I found [the Interfaith Family Project of Greater Washington], I found the community that I myself had been searching for all my life: a community where interfaith marriage was the norm. A community where no one would challenge my right, or the right of my children, to claim Judaism. . . . And, finally, a community where I felt my family could be at the center rather than on the periphery.[5]

The good news is that no longer are the Interfaith Family Project of Greater Washington and a few like-minded groups solely the ones focusing on the needs of interfaith families, but many American Jewish communities are as well. As a matter of both justice and effectiveness, our communal institutions should do even more to reach out to and care for those who do not have two Jewish parents, are not Ashkenazic, are not straight, and are not partnered. We should even look beyond people who identify themselves as Jews for life.

Much as we should continue honoring membership in a people, we should also acknowledge how people can be Jewish, do Jewish, and experience Jewish in more ephemeral ways. Those who love Katzinger's Deli in Columbus, Ohio, might want to feel a sense of Ashkenazic homecoming only for a single meal. Those who meditate with the Institute for Jewish Spirituality online might only seek Chasidic notions of connection to God for the span of a meditation session. Korean Americans and Chinese Americans who grew up with volumes of the Talmud in translation might want to read of rabbinic wisdom for an afternoon, without committing to a lifetime of yeshiva learning. Black Pentecostal Christians might wish to find resonance in the Passover seder as a ritual of liberation, without seeking to join the people that came into its own through the Exodus.

Much as Americans of all backgrounds partake in yoga, which is rooted in Hindu tradition, or draw inspiration from Buddhist thinker Thich Nhat Hanh, so too should we entertain the possibility that Jewish ideas, practices, histories, and ways of being might be shared as a wisdom tradition that is open to all.[6] Complementing the tradition upheld strongly by our ancestors, who were forced into shtetls and ghettos, is a wisdom tradition that can be embraced by all and help people navigate this time of unprecedented complexity in human life. When some leaders of Hillel speak of "doing Jewish," they typically do not speak only of Jews.[7] When Clal—The National Jewish Center for Learning and Leadership speaks of "Jewish as a public good,"[8] it does not mean solely for those whose belonging is affirmed by Orthodox interpretations of Jewish law.

The desperate hunger for age-old wisdom, inspiration, and rootedness in a time of unparalleled flux means that we need to open up to the possibility that in addition to Jews by Choice, Jews of Color, and Jews of every background and combination possible in the realm of human life, there may be a growing number of people who are Jewishly inspired but are not genetically Jewish, do not evince a desire to convert, and are not drawn to other typical formulations of our tradition. In time, people from myriad cultural and ethnic backgrounds might be Muslims, Hindus, Buddhists, Sikhs, or humanists, yet seek to experience that which we call Jewish. Like the houseguest who is not part of the household, like the resident who does not become a citizen,[9] like the community visitor who does not become a community member, we need to celebrate a growing array of Jewish experiences and ways of being. These are more varied and expansive than earlier manifestations of Jewish life and will require a new vocabulary that acknowledges multiple paths to doing Jewish and forms of identification within each one. Rather than providing a path *out* of Judaism as an ethnicity, they will provide a path *into* relationship with Jewish wisdom, beliefs, spiritual practices, culture, and community.

As Rabbi Irwin Kula and Professor Vanessa Ochs reflect, "Our sturdy Jewish tradition allows us freedom to experiment, innovate, and be expressive in Jewish language. Jews have always developed liturgical and ritual responses to their lives."[10] Insofar as Jewish is a language of spiritual expression, in addition to all else, it can be one accessible to all. We suspect that the new Jewish awakening will be shaped not only by those on the edge of Jewish life, but also by the growing ranks of people beyond the edge of our sometimes narrow communal self-definitions. This may be a path toward self-actualization. Our wisdom can indeed be a "light unto the world,"[11] if only we allow it to shine beyond the walls of the institutions and community buildings that seek to contain it at the expense of those who do not venture in.

An ethos of pluralism will enable these new boundaries of Jewish experience to combine with existing ones. More than simply affirming the validity of a Jewish denomination other than one's own, this will entail affirming that a person can be Jewishly inspired, in any number of dimensions, in an authentic, knowledgeable way. People need not view Jewish solely as a marker of identity. Not only could a person be Reform, Conservative, Reconstructionist, Renewal, Modern Orthodox, or ultra-Orthodox (and any number of subgenres therein), but also a gender-fluid, Black atheist or developing a *tikun midot* practice to improve one's humane qualities. One might live as a Jew but never formally convert. One could be a passionate religious Zionist, immigrant Jew by Choice with a meditation practice and a yearning for a personal relationship to God. One could be ultra-Orthodox in practice, a deist in theology, lacking in any Jewish ancestry, and an expert in rabbinic commentaries from the purported twelfth-century atheist rabbi par excellence Moses Maimonides. One could also be a Hindu who has adopted a traditional Shabbat practice to unplug from a stressful week. This is about encouraging not appropriation, but rather appreciation, with the confidence that our tradition has much to offer others.

As the approaches to Jewish experience broaden radically, our Diaspora will require an equally radical ethos of intra-religious pluralism, which affirms the inherent good of Jewish experiences in any number of areas of life, without expecting lifetime membership of the sort once assumed to be cast in stone. Rather than being a path away from Judaism, broadening the scope of accepted practice and actively bringing Jewish ideas and practices to more people will provide a springboard for welcoming many more people who seek to forever entwine their lives with the Jewish people, the Jewish community, and ways of life inspired by Jewish tradition.

CHAPTER 18

Belonging

The outside world is so hospitable to Jews that Jewish communities can no longer rely on external hostility to make themselves a haven for Jews. The Jewish awakening reflects their need to provide a multitude of deeper experiences, which each individual can knit together into a self-reinforcing whole—a lifestyle.

In his book *After Heaven,* Robert Wuthnow explores decades of research into the trends of religion in America. He notes that most Americans fall into two categories: "dwellers" and "seekers." Those who find meaning and purpose in stability are dwellers. Those who find meaning and purpose in the journey—across shifting landscapes and beyond safe walls—or who have not landed in their preferred dwelling place are seekers. Within Jewish history, we encounter both. Dwellers embrace Temple religion and the faith of kings and priests. Seekers favor Tabernacle religion and the faith of pilgrims, prophets, and mystics.[1]

We bear two ideals, propelled over and over again in our tradition to leave home, only to come home again. We leave a promised land, only to strive to return. Our patriarchs and matriarchs enter and leave and enter and leave. We are the wanderers, and we are the builders. We retain the tradition of the Tabernacle, carrying God's presence in the midst of seeking, and we hold fast to the memory of the iconic Temple, a fixed house for God. Ours is a perpetual story of leaving in order to return. The challenge is that, upon arrival, we never manage to stay put.

Nearly a century ago, Rabbi Mordecai Kaplan helped found the Jewish Center on Eighty-Sixth Street in New York City. Kaplan made this ten-story structure into "a shul with a pool and a school."[2] At that time, he knew that the synagogue had to both create community and help integrate American Jewry into civic life. Synagogues needed to become multifaceted clearing-houses of culture and connection, each one a true Jewish community center—a social, spiritual, and communal home for recent immigrants, who still felt like outsiders in this new land.[3] This model filled the emerging needs of the Jewish community at the time.

Fifty years ago, nearly 70 percent of American Jews belonged to a synagogue, with facilities bursting at the seams with demand.[4] Today that number hovers around 30 percent.[5] At the same time, as some of our teachers have noted, 94 percent of Jews are "proud to be Jewish."[6] This suggests that institutional affiliation is no longer a prerequisite for affirming Jewishness.[7] Kaplan's vision of the synagogue as a Jewish intermediary with the broader world worked in a time when Jews could not afford, gain access to, or find interest in what secular society had to offer. Those conditions from a century ago do not exist today. The same mismatch between human need and institutional offering that inspired Kaplan may be seen again (albeit in different form), demanding a new reconstruction of communal life to fit the present needs of American Jewry.

We now live at a time of greater specialization. Organizations offering meaning in life abound and are designed for this era of seekers, from book clubs and Pilates studios, to meetup groups, online gatherings of trivia aficionados, and workshops for craft beer making. Today's gourmet dinner is likely to feature fish from the fish market, cheese from the specialty cheese store, and produce from the farmers market, rather than conventional offerings of each from a single mass-market supermarket. This is increasingly becoming true in the Jewish world as well.

The buffet approach of programs at many synagogues and community centers struggles to compete. Specialized institutions for Mussar or Talmud, social justice and Israel advocacy, Jewish cooking and Jewish dating draw numerous adherents because they serve a specific programmatic mission. Jewish communities and organizations should create or bring in the best offerings that meet specific needs. Jewish communities must provide deeper experiences, which each empowered individual brings together into a bespoke whole—that is, a lifestyle.

One community might focus on mindfulness, immigration rights advocacy, Israeli cuisine, and welcoming Jews by Choice. Another might offer ebullient prayer services, the study of classical Jewish texts, and travel to Jewish Diasporas worldwide. A third might champion progressive Zionism, youth engagement, and lay empowerment. People would come with a purpose and stay due to a growing sense of belonging if they feel a sense of fitting in with people who share similar interests. They might underestimate the value of community in the abstract but come to recognize its significance as a source of meaning and social sustenance in practice.

The Springtide Research Institute studied loneliness among thirteen- to twenty-five-year-olds in Gen Z and identified the factors of religious community that were meaningful to young people in what they termed "America's loneliest generation":

> We discovered that young people who have a relationship with at least one trusted adult in a religious institution are more trusting, less isolated, less stressed, and more confident about their future. In other words, attending religious services does not reduce loneliness, but a relationship with even one trusted adult in a religious organization does.[8]

Religious communities can create a space for the kind of trusting relationships that are increasingly rare and critical for mental health and well-being. Common causes in a community setting create the basis for people to forge those relationships.

A number of start-ups, many of which were described in part 3 of this book, are reimagining the forms that community can take. Many have focused on the young professional demographic, as the gap between college graduation and finding a partner in life (if they choose to find a partner at all) continues to widen.[9] With more choices about how to conceptualize family or chosen family, these communities are gradually expanding to serve multiple generations at the same time. Likewise, they are recognizing the multiplicity of ways to be Jewish and to connect Jewishly.

At the same time, long-standing communities may seize the opportunity to innovate in transformational ways. Legacy institutions that require formal membership and brick-and-mortar buildings can become incubators of communal change on a scale that few newcomers can. Rabbi Sid Schwartz documents this in his book *Jewish Megatrends*:

> Although the fledgling programs [of a grassroots nature] are capturing Jewish millennials more successfully than are more established institutions, Federations, JCCs, and synagogues have infrastructure, facilities, expertise, and access to financial resources that the younger Jewish organizations have no ability to replicate.[10]

Jewish social entrepreneurs have a mission, while long-standing organizations have more financial and operational stability.

Rabbi Paul Yedwab,[11] from Temple Israel of West Bloomfield, Michigan, sees even more of a role for innovation from within: seeding successor institutions. He uses the analogy of Hudson's, a department store in the Detroit area, and the far more widely known start-up that it incubated: Target. Yedwab reflects:

> Suddenly, Hudson's disappeared, seemingly into thin air. As it turns out, however, the Dayton Hudson Corporation did not go away. Instead, Hudson's had inserted into the market its own competitor, creating what is known in the business world as a "disruptor." You've probably heard of that start-up; it's called Target. Eventually, the disruptor grew to become the second-largest discount retailer in the world, overtaking its parent company to the point where the mall stores were sold off and the name of the corporation changed.[12]

Mainstream synagogues, federations, and Jewish community centers hold the potential to innovate at an unparalleled scale. Instead of clinging to past glory, they can recognize themselves as department stores with the resources and supply chains to found an Amazon.

Yedwab gives examples of how large, well-established communities can seed movement-building initiatives.[13] The country's largest Reform synagogue, Temple Israel in West Bloomfield, Michigan, established "The Well," an initiative to transform young professional engagement and pioneer "crowd-raising" as a central source of funding; the musically innovative "Shabbat unplugged" service; the first social service agency in a synagogue; the first mikveh in a Reform congregation; the first PowerPoint prayer book; the first Jewish bereavement support group. Much as disruptors learn about the marketplace, so too has Temple Israel as an incubator.

Most striking is Yedwab's description of Temple Israel's culture: one of collaboration, nonhierarchical leadership, forthrightness, and fearlessness in experimentation. In contrast to many other large synagogues, he reports that it has no senior rabbi, limited divisions between clergy and lay leadership, and a focus on ideas over personalities.

Whether or not Temple Israel will exist in another century or become a shell, like Hudson's downtown flagship, its culture will live on in the spiritual ventures it founds.[14] Other major, well-funded synagogues and organizations would do well to follow suit, deemphasizing charismatic leadership and creating a culture of ongoing experimentation—with ample investment in the future, learning from their failures, and using their staying power to keep trying until a successor institution takes root.

While few can retire comfortably by saving just 1 percent of their salaries, most mainstay organizations do not even invest that much in innovation. They should consider whether there is a way to invest 5 percent or 10 percent or 20 percent of their annual budgets in thoughtful, carefully critiqued experiments that could one day bear fruit. Unless they do, institutional mainstays will continue lumbering along, failing to attract younger cohorts, and following a path of gradual descent. Many are already losing the footrace with low-cost, high-meaning innovators.

In some areas, organizations are stepping up to incubate these initiatives and cultivate new leaders who can better serve specific interest groups and cohorts. After witnessing many young Jews in Portland, Oregon, struggling to find a place of Jewish belonging, Eleyna Fugman felt a growing sense of urgency:

> When we tried to enter these spaces, we had the sense of feeling unseen as young Jews, queer and trans Jews, multiracial Jews—or we would struggle with feeling like we did not know enough, having grown up in interfaith families or raised outside of Jewish homes or communities. We sought places where we could bring our whole selves, and the solution seemed to be that we needed to build those spaces for ourselves.[15]

Fugman saw a number of young Jews trying to create their own Jewish communities, but lacking in resources, support, and mentorship. In 2016, she cofounded TischPDX in Portland to address and overcome these barriers.

TischPDX incubates young adult leaders from marginalized identities— including queer, interfaith, and Black/Indigenous/people of color—who have demonstrated a passion for community and empowerment. Through a sixteen-month leadership incubator, these emerging community creators receive fifty hours of Jewish education and skill building, with peer support, professional mentorship, and stipends. "Our model is building leadership from the outside in," Fugman explains. "Instead of providing programming that marginalized Jews might come to, we are going to marginalized Jews and saying, 'What are you doing? How can we help you?'"[16]

TischPDX has now graduated two cohorts of fellows, and they have sparked hundreds of gatherings. It models how a hub of leadership empowerment may establish new networks of Jewish community that can transform the margins of Jewish life into centers in their own right. It may also presage a new model for synagogue life, centered on empowerment, spiritual inspiration, and the cultivation of leaders, who create other circles of Jewish community. Synagogues can become the gathering places for a network of smaller communities based around identities and affinities.

CHAPTER 19

Joining Together

With the growth of technology as a means to offer education, allow worship, and establish community, geographic barriers fade and smaller communities can knit themselves together across state lines and denominations.

According to Brandeis University's 2020 American Jewish Population Project, one in five American Jews live outside the top forty metro areas of the country.[1] With more than a million American Jews geographically unserved by mainstay organizations, the Jewish Federation of North America established its own Network of Independent Communities, weaving together three hundred geographically disparate small (often rural) Jewish communities.[2] In this network formation, resources are shared and mutually shouldered, giving volunteer leaders tools for engagement, leadership, and financial stewardship. The initiatives of these small communities then spread across the network, conferring on members a sense of collective purpose even when they're geographically distant. In turn, this network can inspire national giving, drawing on philanthropic support to bolster the entire network and the more than two hundred thousand Jews served by the web of communities.

During her final year of rabbinical school at the Jewish Theological Seminary, Rabbi Rachel Isaacs heard a leader give this suggestion for the Conservative movement: "The future of the American Jewish community is in twelve major cities, and we need to find a way to let the rest go."[3] After spending time as a student rabbi in Waterville, Maine, Rabbi Isaacs saw the impact such an approach would have on real lives and the nature of American Judaism as a whole:

Whether he knew it or not, this leader was not just proposing a cost-effective strategy for our movement's future, he was making a claim about who deserves Jewish life. In effect, if not in intent, he claimed that you must live in an economically prosperous area in order to enjoy the support and services of Jewish community. His dismissal of communities like Waterville inspired my wife, Mel, and me to begin our life here, and forge a path that made small town Jewish life sustainable, vibrant, and relevant.[4]

Rabbi Isaacs partnered with Dr. Rabbi David Freidenreich, chair of the Jewish Studies Program at Colby College, to create the Center for Small Town Jewish Life. Rabbi Isaacs helped shape a new role, jointly serving as rabbi of Beth Israel Congregation, faculty member in the Jewish Studies Department of Colby College, and director of CSTJL. Not only does such a structure help with the cost allocation of rabbinic leadership, but each of these organizations then amplifies each other's work.

Colby College provides academic course access to CSTJL, Beth Israel Congregation provides spiritual resources and worship services, and CSTJL helps gather multiple generations from across the entire state to share in Jewish-centered programs. For seven years running, CSTJL hosted an annual Maine Conference for Jewish Life, bringing hundreds together for learning and community engagement.[5] Through youth group programs and the Funtensive, a youth camp hosted through Temple Beth El in Augusta, CSTJL weaves Jewish communities together into a network of connection. Rather than denominational framing of relationship, Rabbi Isaacs helped to knit together resources and smaller hubs of Jewish life into a statewide consortium.

In 2000, Macy Hart founded the Goldring/Woldenberg Institute of Southern Jewish Life in Jackson, Mississippi, creating a hub for thirteen southern states and establishing a network of cross-denominational services and resources. From cultural programming to educational offerings, ISJL helps spread the impact of experiences engaging just small numbers of Jews to wider geographic regions. It also helps support a team of "Rabbis on the Road," providing access to worship and life-cycle events for areas that cannot support full-time clergy. Through the use of online learning and in-person gatherings, and defraying costs across the network, ISJL serves more than one hundred different communities and reaches thousands of children through religious school curriculum.[6] Additionally, the institute helps elevate awareness of the vast Jewish history in the region and even offers oral histories, an encyclopedia of southern Jewish communities, and virtual tours and road trips[7] to encourage engagement with and awareness of the Jewish South.

These examples of Jewish networks reflect new ways of bringing together and extending the reach of disparate Jewish communities. With the growth of technology as a feasible way to make education and worship services accessible and match resources with needs, geographic barriers fade and smaller communities can join together across state lines, denominations, and any other barriers. Funders supporting CSTJL and ISJL may see their donations engaging people across large regions, and congregations can harness their particular strengths and use them as assets for others. The focus on connection over ideology provides other benefits as well. ISJL created a trans-denominational curriculum, used in Conservative, Reform, and unaffiliated communities across the region.

CHAPTER 20

Feeling at Home

Many will place a continued premium on in-person experiences and community, as loneliness inspires not only the search for meaning, but the quest for deeper relationships.

As Andrew Solomon points out in his book *Far from the Tree*, the formation of identity takes place in two ways. Vertical identities are those attributes and values passed from one generation to the next; horizontal identities are those fostered by one's peer group. Ethnicity and nationality tend to be examples of the former, while cultural identity and political affiliation tend to exemplify the latter. Solomon posits that rifts occur between generations when identity moves from vertical framing to horizontal, as a person's sense of self shifts away from a home of origin and toward a new center of belonging.[1]

Rising generations have not adopted their parents' and grandparents' models of community and are instead creating new ones for themselves.[2] We believe this is now occurring across American Judaism, notably in the interplay between home and spiritual community. Rather than joining synagogues, a growing number of people are creating prayer spaces in their homes, gathering with friends, or turning their homes into synagogues.

The Chabad House has become the archetypical home-based center of spiritual life. Over one thousand have sprung up across the United States, with seed funding for husband-wife teams to create communities in both population centers and far-flung areas of the country.[3] These entrepreneurial and familial partners model traditional family life, while actively welcoming all who seek Jewish ritual, connection, and community. Dr. Steven Windmueller chronicles Chabad's "ten core elements for success," which "begin with one Jew at a time" and rely on the need to "meet clients where they are."[4] In addition to being highly visible and remaining in the public square, Chabad Houses provide emotional connection and the context for forming deep relationships in a society often fraught with superficiality.

Chabad Houses have programs and activities that do not require deep Jewish knowledge, such as drinks in the sukkah or a comedy night for Purim. Likewise, they create a real sense of home for people far from relatives. A home-cooked Shabbat meal can fill the stomach and warm the heart, enabling disconnected Jews to feel like part of something bigger, rooted in history but with the comforts of modern life.

Building on the successes of this home-based model are a host of more spiritually and socially progressive alternatives. Moishe House began as an experimental community in California and has blossomed into a network of spaces around the world. Instead of relying on a husband-wife leadership team, they provide subsidized rent for Jewish professionals, with the expectation that the shared home will become a space for Jewish programs, events, ideas, and life. Moishe House engages more than seventy thousand young adults through twelve thousand programs annually.[5] It creates space for young lay leaders to find their voices and welcome their peers: "Moishe House is now the global leader in peer-led Jewish young adult engagement. . . . All programming is planned and executed by their peers, creating countless opportunities for young adults to connect with their own Jewish identities, their friends, and their wider communities."[6] Moishe House expanded and broadened its reach by merging with Hillel International's Base Movement, a network of rabbinic home-based engagement. Now Moishe House melds peer empowerment with rabbinic resources outside the traditional Jewish synagogue structure.[7]

This ethos of empowerment recognizes both the power of peer-to-peer interactions in identity formation and the need to allow the next generation to define the Jewish home, Jewish life, and Jewish points of connection. It is poised for rapid growth, particularly as it draws on its growing base of alumni and supports the co-creation of programs and spaces at more stages of adult life.

Alongside the Chabad House and Moishe House model resides Beloved, a network that relies on spiritual leaders in home-based communities, while giving voice to laypeople and those becoming more engaged with

110

Jewish life. Rabbi Sara Luria and her husband Isaac Luria piloted this approach in Brooklyn and then empowered other spiritual leaders to create spiritually progressive "Chabad-style" houses of ritual and relationship.[8]

Rabbi Luria reflected on her efforts:

> We created a home-based experiment in Jewish life and community. What that means is that we wanted to figure out if we could bring together the strands of food and ritual and a feeling of comfort and love and familiarity and Jewish tradition into one place, and that's why we chose a home.[9]

By seeking to evoke the feelings of home—care, support, embrace, nurturing—the Beloved network has grown in scope and scale and portends further changes to the ways in which progressive Jews, including those rooted within particular denominations, gather and celebrate life together.

Another hybrid model, often connected to synagogue and home, is the "independent minyan." Rabbi Elie Kaunfer examines prayer and social groups in his book *Empowered Judaism: What Independent Minyanim Can Teach Us about Building Vibrant Jewish Communities.*[10] Between 2000 and 2009, more than sixty of these groups sprang up, with dozens more following suit thereafter.[11] Rabbi Kaunfer describes them as "led by volunteers, with no paid clergy," lacking denominational affiliation, and meeting at least once a month.[12] Some rent space or lead programs in collaboration with Jewish institutions, and many offer classes to support soulful prayer. Some experience rapid growth, while others expand more gradually, each providing particular choices of prayer and experience and focusing on relationship-building.

Rabbi Kaunfer concludes that "vibrant, egalitarian, spirited prayer communities are now possible in the twenty-first century. . . . They took the power of traditional Judaism and made it compelling and energizing."[13] In their successful effort to empower young Jews to reclaim Judaism, community, and spiritual practice, they raise the question of how the American Diaspora can scale opportunities for education and empowerment. In many respects, they are the embodiment of awakening and a path to communal revitalization, from the grass roots. They also point to the need for deeper investment in laypeople, whose growth and empowerment have been undermined for the sake of maintaining the spiritual authority of clergy.

For those with less experience or drive to join a community, bespoke, at-home experiences now also abound. The power of the holiday care package or "Shabbat in a Box"[14] can elevate spiritual experiences at home for family and friends. In 2016, Rabbi Noa Kushner and her San Francisco-based Kitchen community founded Hello Mazel as a venture to send the Jewish "hipster care package" to young professionals and other institutionally disconnected Jews across the country.[15] Its Kickstarter campaign garnered over $70,000 in initial funding, with an initial care package for Passover, replete with "delightfully fun, surprising bits of Jewishness" and "a visual and culinary aesthetic from 2016, not 1974."[16] You can now invite friends over, open a care package, and create an instant, pop-up Jewish community.

Many synagogues have since followed suit, especially when the Covid-19 pandemic kept them from gathering with community members in person. The aesthetic experience of Jewish tastes, smells, textures, and art brought people together over time and space. This portends the further devolution of power and points up the importance of immediacy.

One might imagine the possibility of the online platform to bring people together in prayer, study, and community.[17] Jewish community in a box might readily give way to Jewish community on a phone. At the same time, many will place a continued premium on in-person experiences and community, as loneliness inspires not only the search for meaning, but the quest for deeper relationships.

CHAPTER 21

Leading

In elevating laypeople to new roles of prominence,
clergy are not diminished. Rather, they demonstrate
their indispensable place within the Jewish awakening.

If you were to ask a typical American Jew to whom they look for moral, or
even spiritual, leadership, it is unlikely that they would list a single rabbi,
cantor, or Jewish educator. Instead, they might point to one of the top
Jewish columnists: Bari Weiss, Paul Krugman, Brett Stephens, Bill Kristol,
Tom Friedman, Jennifer Senior, or Michelle Goldberg. They might add the
Jewish US Supreme Court justices: Ruth Bader Ginsburg (even posthumous-
ly), Elena Kagan, or Stephen Breyer. They might include authors Cynthia
Ozick, Kyra Davis, or Michael Chabon. Perhaps a leading artist, actor, or
director might be cited: Daveed Diggs, Steven Spielberg, Barbra Streisand,
or Judy Chicago. For some, even complicated political personalities would
make the cut: Ivanka Trump, Senator Bernie Sanders, or Second Gentleman
Douglas Emhoff. Countless others would make the list, depending on whom
one asks. The center of moral authority has so shifted away from the pulpit
that perhaps only historical rabbinical figures would even be contenders.

Rather than wringing our hands at the dearth of larger-than-life moral
superheroes among the rabbinical ranks, it is time to elevate the role of lay
leaders. They are already shaping our self-understanding as a Diaspora and
could come to hold unique roles within communities as teachers, preachers,
and Johnny Appleseeds of innovative ideas. Beyond unofficial communal
think tanks and task forces, these great minds should help guide Jewish
conversations that create new Torah and expand our collective wisdom.

Rabbi Irving "Yitz" Greenberg forecasted the trend in 1987 when he
observed that "each era of Jewish history has generated its own character-

istic cadre. Leadership has gravitated toward those who could cope with the problems of living while addressing, overtly or through their work, the meaning and purpose of being a Jew."[1] In our own era, he saw the rise of laypeople: "Lay leaders appear as normal, everyday people. Their claims are seen thereby as more tentative and more likely to acknowledge others' claims."[2] In leading collaboratively and actively seeking input from others, lay leaders put in place the groundwork for co-creating institutions, which thereby immediately have a built-in following and focus on the needs of people within the Diaspora. They serve human purposes in ways that are shaped by Jewish practices and ideas.

In addition to communal ventures, a growing number of online platforms are lay run and filled with key Jewish content. Creating a bridge of ideas between Israel and the Diaspora—and encouraging a breadth of ideas too rarely seen within political silos in both Israel and the United States— is the thriving news and blogging website the Times of Israel. Founding editor-in-chief David Horovitz[3] reflected on the notion of blending journalistic expertise and the informality of blogging on the same platform, with editorial oversight to avoid hate speech and ensure the quality of contributions. He noted that beyond the nearly fifty journalists on staff, the blog platform disrupted the status quo in Jewish journalism. Approximately ten thousand different people have contributed to the blog, with numbers continuing to rise.[4]

Horovitz acknowledges that the journalism "wouldn't have the same resonance if it wasn't for the blog platform" and that they increasingly intersect. In addition, the twenty-four-hour cycle of blogging around the world requires a great deal from its editorial staff, since "whoever is running the site is the gatekeeper of what we publish" and that "has to be really first class and savvy and skeptical."

The impact on dialogue between Jews around the world has been staggering—notably within the United States. While clergy have long-standing ways of sharing their ideas, the Times of Israel creates a community of contributors, many of whom are not Jewish clergy or even formally lay leaders. Their ability to create content, share ideas, shape discourse, and respond to other blog posts is emblematic of the central role of laypeople as thought leaders.

The website is run *by* laypeople and largely *for* laypeople, who in turn shape ideas in the United States and in communities around the world. The lines of leadership blur as laypeople gain bigger platforms than their clergy counterparts and reflect on issues of spiritual and human concern with growing authority. This mirrors the growing role of lay leaders in Moishe Houses in planning programs and building community; in Limmud North America and its festivals of lay-driven learning; in centers of learning at Hadar and the Pardes Institute; at Jewish federations; and at countless synagogues across the country, some of which are thriving even in the absence of formal clergy.

New paths to Jewish wisdom are extending opportunities for laypeople. ALEPH and the Kohenet Hebrew Priestess Institute provide part-time paths toward ordination for people who might never seek out formal pulpits but want to be knowledgeable leaders of community in all its manifestations. Lay clergy institutes[5] create hybrid roles for those who seek to take on limited pastoral, teaching, and preaching responsibilities in synagogues that joyfully elevate new leadership.

Rabbis and cantors, therefore, redouble their role as teachers. Rabbi Elie Kaunfer suggests that this is their future: to seek space not simply for their own exercise of leadership, but also for other leaders, whom they empower, inspire, teach, and mentor. Much as priestly rituals, which were centered on ancient spiritual leaders, have given way to the rise of rabbis as teachers, clergy today revert to the role of teachers from that of "symbolic exemplar"[6] and path-breaker for social acceptance of a community of immigrants. In elevating laypeople to new roles of prominence, clergy do not diminish themselves, but rather demonstrate their indispensable place within the Jewish awakening.

Co-creating a New Center

The American Diaspora needs a new infrastructure of connection and relationship-building, one centered on people rather than the preservation of institutions.

The most practiced Jewish rite today is the Passover seder.[1] The early rabbis proclaimed that one must tell the story so it moves "from slavery to freedom, from sorrow to joy, from mourning to a festival, from darkness to a great light, and from enslavement to redemption." These early rabbis also required that we do so annually to understand the cycles of our journey as people—and as a people.

Yet the retelling of the Exodus did not begin with a Haggadah written to guide the annual Passover seder. It did not even begin with Moses's recapitulation of his journey with the Israelites in the Book of Deuteronomy, but rather within the Book of Exodus itself. Not long after the Israelites traverse the Sea of Reeds, God commands Moses to tell the children of Israel, "You have seen what I did to the Egyptians, how I bore you on eagles' wings and brought you to Me."[2]

What does this new narrative mean to a group of people who just trudged on miraculously dry land across the Sea of Reeds? According to commentators, Rashi among them, the eagle is the only creature that carries its young on its back, because it flies so high that other birds do not pose a threat from above. While most fledglings look down in flight, young eagles look up.

So it is for the Israelites after the Exodus. Their path to freedom enabled them to look up for the first time and behold the wonders that existed beyond their bondage in Egypt.

And so too is it for the American Diaspora right now. If only we awaken to the possibilities before us.

Like the Jewish awakening nearly a century and a half ago, the emergent trends are not defined by those at the center, but rather are being sparked by people who may feel as if they are at the fringe of Jewish leadership and power: women, LGBTQ Jews, Jews of Color, Jews by Choice, immigrants, people whose ancestry is only partially Jewish, and laypeople without formal credentials.

Centralized power structures and organizations will continue their decline, as will professionals and philanthropists who seek to maintain the status quo. As the center falls away, we might for a time return to something closer to the early centuries of rabbinic Judaism, in which loose groupings of peers, teachers, and students study together and create novel approaches to Jewish practice, centered around human need and common purpose. They will ask questions of our community, interrogate tradition, and develop new paths to self-understanding and spiritual growth. But as we are already seeing, these informal study circles, activist groups, and centers of leadership will coalesce into networks, movements, and new organizations.

Much as one might be tempted to mourn the loss of the central institutions of Diaspora and bemoan their demise as symptoms of communal decline, their decline and fall should be viewed more neutrally—or even with outright optimism—as a sign of spiritual yearning yet unanswered by existing institutions and compelling us to build anew. Like Rabbi Akiva laughing with hope at the ruins of the Temple in Jerusalem, so much of what now fades is a measure of past success and future possibility. Dr. Rosabeth Moss Kanter of Harvard Business School posits that the middle mark of change tends to be where gloom darkens perspective and many lose sight of the renewal that waits to unfold. Dubbing this "Kanter's Law," she suggests, "Everything looks like a failure in the middle."[3] What distinguishes visionary leadership is the capacity to look up and see a story beyond the failure. "Renew the dream, regroup to remove roadblocks, surround yourself with supporters who cheer you on, and stick with it."[4]

We live now in the middle, as former structures fall away and many feel that our inherited narrative has somehow failed. If we look backward on the moments of consolidation and fragmentation, of fractures and renewals, we may glean the wisdom to look up and beyond to see a larger story of awakening. Our people has realized its dreams of integration and can now look beyond self-defense toward self-actualization. We see a return to classical rabbinic texts and thought as a means by which people nearing the top of Maslow's famed hierarchy of needs can continue their ascent.[5] We see a return to spiritual practices at home and even in the public square, where often one finds safety to practice Judaism openly and share traditions with people beyond the fold.

We also see the rapid rise of Jews by Choice, as well as people who turn to Jewish ideas and traditions more informally to respond to their needs or help them navigate a society fraught with technological and social change. We note the fluidity of identity, the presence of multiple senses of belonging, and the reality that some might view Judaism as a spiritual tool kit or source of wisdom, among many they scour for truth and insight. Rather than denigrating these approaches, we should view them with wonder. Judaism is now so integrated into American society that its reach transcends thought leaders and pundits, power brokers and culture icons, punchy Yiddish idioms and trendy Israeli cuisine. It is coming to be seen as an authentically American tradition, interwoven into the fabric of American society itself.

As more and more people engage with Torah, ritual, and the rabbinic process of holding in tension multiple simultaneous competing values, the more Torah itself will grow and the more our American Diaspora will grow in self-understanding and self-defined purpose. Our fellow travelers will come to guide our path and ask questions that biological Jews might never have otherwise inquired about—and come to define our diasporic approaches. Those on this edge of Jewish life are already awakening us all to what might be possible and demonstrating the extent to which our "core" so often fails to meet our needs.

Professor Richard Bulliet describes a similar phenomenon in Islam, when rapid expansion brought it to what is modern-day Iran and Iraq in the seventh century. In his book *Islam: The View from the Edge*,[6] Bulliet suggests that new converts and those newly introduced to Islam played a key role in defining its spiritual contours by asking questions about practice and provenance. They relied on networks of scholars and created a synthesis of ideas that continues to define Muslim practice in many parts of the world.

With the loosening of institutional constraints, the growth of converts, and the awakening of those already Jewishly connected, the American

Diaspora is poised for a similar synthesis. Teachings that once seemed arcane will come into dialogue with deeply human concerns, as seekers demand[7] more of Jewish ideas and thereby bring forth more from them. In doing so, they might unearth new means to unite broad swaths of our Diaspora and the countless people across our society who are moved or impacted by America's great Jewish community. In liberating ourselves from preconceived notions of Jewish life and practice, we can awaken to the possibility of what lies ahead.

At the same time, we need to retain an awareness of the past and an appreciation for tradition. Starting from scratch is not an awakening as much as a rejection of all that was—good, bad, and complicated. Even as we seek new formulations for Jewish culture, ritual, identity, and belonging, we do so in ongoing dialogue with our past and with tradition.

The tractate *Eduyot* of the Mishnah, a rabbinic text codified in the third century of the Common Era, commends us for retaining minority viewpoints in the course of rabbinic debates, both so that we can revert to earlier perspectives and so that we can avoid laborious discussions over issues that we have already resolved.[8] We would do well to affirm this in our own era. We should create radical new expressions of Jewish life, all the while charting our trajectory from earlier ways of being and doing Jewish. We should make space for new voices, new ideas, new ways of belonging, accessing spiritual wisdom, and finding purpose, without summarily discarding those that become less central to our Diaspora. The variation of practice from which we draw serves as a font of inspiration today. Its replacement with a new monoculture would undermine the essence of our multivocal tradition.

In his 2010 study of new Jewish leaders, Jack Wertheimer concludes, "Not only is the map of organized Jewish life changing but small organizations and programs geared to every conceivable niche population are multiplying, resulting in a community that increasingly lacks a center. Fragmentation and localism are the order of the day."[9] Here is also the story of expansion, of new doors of belonging and new forms of Jewish community. The terminology and edifices that defined generations of Jewish life may be fading, but our future calls with excitement for new language and structure to forge a new center of American Judaism.

A Jewish awakening is rising around us. Let us behold all who now empower others to be creators in this new frontier. Let us welcome them, learn from them, teach them, dream with them—and co-create a new center. It will take time, energy, debate, experimentation, and failure. But we are poised to venture beyond the wildest dreams of our forebears into an era of widespread access to wisdom, collective empowerment, and a purpose that moves from surviving to thriving. Moses dreamed of a time when all people would be prophets, making Judaism a collective, building community and spreading wisdom. We believe that age is now before us.

It begins by counting people in, instead of counting them out—or, at the very least, counting with a purpose. If our narrative of decline and collapse was amplified by the 1990 National Jewish Population Survey, it was because our numbers became a purpose unto themselves, when our tradition has always been intended to serve human needs.[10] The survey triggered trauma-laden fears of a "second Holocaust" and reinforced age-old tropes about the "decline of generations," while failing to uncover what did animate people Jewishly. Survey authors assumed that intermarriage would lead to demographic decline and gathered scholars to study a ship that they long thought would sink. Many others followed suit, gawking at what they thought would be a listing ship. The boat is still afloat and sailing quite well. But we have wasted untold time, energy, and resources focusing on its inevitable end and—in some cases—trying in vain to bail out the water that was hardly gathering beneath its hull to begin with.

An immediate corrective resides in the very source of the problem: a census of Jewish life, rather than of its undoing. We need to know what Jews value—and who else values Judaism. How are Jewish ideas and practices permeating wider society? Who still holds The Diary of a Young Girl by Anne Frank to be their most cherished book? Who observes some kind of Shabbat to mark the end of the workweek? Who has been inspired by a trip to Israel? Who sat shiva upon the loss of a loved one? Who has Jewish family members or friends and looks to them for spiritual sustenance?

If our purpose is to inspire Jewish life and people to embrace Jewish wisdom anew, whether or not they seek permanent membership within our people, we need a census of the practices, ideas, and ways of being that give life to so many. As Hedy Peyser often asked of volunteers at the senior center where she worked, "What would you love to do?" We must prioritize finding the purposes that unite people in doing Jewish and in encountering Judaism as a verb rather than a noun.

With a bouquet of purposes now revealed, we can get to work. The American Diaspora needs a new infrastructure of connection and relationship-building, one centered on people, rather than the preservation of institutions. As people again draw on Judaism to meet the needs of contemporary life, we awaken to an ancient trope: nestled within the story of decline is the beginning of revival. This is the story before us.

A Call to Action

As our ancestors have done for millennia, we leave that which has been familiar in search of a new future.

Awaken, my dear one, my fair one, and go. . . .
The rains have passed and have gone.
The blossoms are again seen in our land. The time of pruning
has come. We hear the voice of the turtledove in our land.
Green figs are forming on the tree, the vines are in blossom
and giving off their scent. Awaken, my dear one; my fair
one, and go.

—SONG OF SONGS 2:10-13

Spiritual search and romantic relationships require courage of heart from each of us if we are to depart from the norms previously known in pursuit of greater fulfillment. Realizing the promise of a new Jewish awakening will require such bravery. We can feel its energy all around us in the people connected to Jewish traditions and ideas, but we have not yet created communities and ecosystems that harness its power. Yet our awakening has already begun at the edges of the American Diaspora. To bring it to the center requires a rethinking of our existing institutions and experimentation with new models of community. So, too, must it have a depth of love for our fellow explorers, which embraces risk and centers on human needs.

We cannot yet see all the ways in which the awakening will create fundamental shifts in how we gather,[1] what we emphasize within Jewish practice, who is welcomed into the wide tent of pluralism, and how we organize our resources and power for the greater good. Yet there are principles that can define our process of discovery as we awaken and depart from a status quo that has served our American Diaspora well for over a century. As in prior generations, human need drives social change, so we articulate these principles in the context of the felt needs of our time.

First, we see a need for people-centered Judaism and, more specifically, to center on those who are alive today. Our love of long-standing institutions and nostalgic ways of being is not an act of vanity, but one that honors the courage and wisdom of those who enabled our existence today, a chain of both tradition and innovation. Yet, our gaze backward ought not interfere with our capacity to experience the needs of today and to envision a future that calls us to responsibility and purpose. As earlier generations reached toward a vision of betterment, so are we called to do the same. Just as we may celebrate their capacity to hear the cries of need and shape new modes of community and practice in response, we may don that mantle ourselves today. Those who came before us are our enduring memories, but they cannot be our ever-evolving purpose.

Second, we see a need to invest in relationships, in knitting people together with thick and authentic connection. In the face of the modern plagues of loneliness and isolation, we may shape ever-expansive narratives that invite the need for others. As *chavruta*, learning in fellowship, became the pathway to wisdom and God, we may bring this Jewish modality into the center of community life, seeing relationship-building as our primary purpose. In so doing, we will see diversity of identity and ideology as a source of growth, rather than a threat to integrity, and become all the wiser for it. This means, in narrative, structure, and leadership, proactively including the many people who had been relegated to the periphery of Jewish life. In particular, this means empowering and embracing Jews of Color, three-quarters of whom feel pressed to explain their identities in Jewish contexts,[2] as well as women, LGBTQ Jews, Jews by Choice, those considering conversion, people connected through family or friendship to Jews, and individuals informally exploring Jewish practices and traditions.

Third, we see a need to embrace a radical notion of intrareligious pluralism, which focuses on actions over identities. Prior generations successfully lowered the barriers to belonging and access for American Jews, and now—through marriage, friendship, and work—these social barriers fade more and more. This is not to say that Jews should in any way ignore norms of *halachah* (Jewish law), but to suggest that we can all buy into the notion that more people sincerely engaged with Jewish ideas, spiritual practices, and community is an inherent good. In actively elevating Judaism as a wisdom tradition, accessible to all, we not only reduce the ignorance that drives hate, but amplify the paths of belonging Judaism may offer. Our focus should be on doing Jewish, not simply being Jewish in a passive way that prioritizes ancestry over action.

Fourth, we see a need for new financial models that enable more people to connect to community and organization. Many synagogues and Jewish organizations still maintain a membership model centered around household makeup, rather than need or desire. By defining membership by whether one is partnered or not, or with children or not, we define value by marital or parental status and imply that such status is the sole lens through which to experience Judaism. Instead, we see a call for a model centered around need, based on interest, life stage, and affinities. As witnessed within nearly every other industry, we see a move away from one-size-fits-all membership models and toward more agency to shape financial relationship to felt need and value. The current trend toward voluntary dues to synagogues[3] only makes more transparent the same membership model of the past, in which the generous few subsidize the many. We see a more radical new financial model coming, one that does not create financial barriers to belonging or consign us to transactional relationships in community. In turn, synagogues will need to glean data to prioritize their resources around the community's needs—say, by offering more home-centered activities—rather than trying to impose the institution's needs on the community. Greater financial data may in turn allow for better financial transparency, helping nurture a more accurate understanding of the value of access to American Judaism and then lead to more paths to expand such financial access.

Fifth, we see a need to harness the expertise within our current organizations and put it to use seeding innovation. The dichotomy between Jewish "start-up" and "legacy" institutions is unhelpful, as some long-standing institutions remain dynamic, while many newcomers retain outdated structures and assumptions about power. Mainstay institutions can serve as incubators of change, funding innovative upstarts and supporting their leaders. Established institutions and philanthropies can also gather communal funds to train and equip spiritual entrepreneurs—perhaps reducing investment in buildings and other unnecessary overhead expenses, and incubating the new ideas that will foster further growth within legacy organizations. Jewish start-ups can avoid the pitfalls of mission creep and the curse of trying to meet all the needs of their constituents by partnering with other organizations and creating new networks and coalitions that together form a tapestry of offerings. Start-ups would likewise do well to study mainstays, learning both from their mistakes and their origins as start-ups decades ago. As the pace of social change accelerates, so will the need for investment in research and development, ensuring that the work of culture change and need-centered priority remains at the forefront of both mainstays and start-ups alike.

Sixth, we see a need to better distribute communal power. At present, many of the ideas and organizational innovations are coming from the periphery, but the funds and formal structures of leadership remain at the center. This mismatch keeps us from harnessing the boldest ideas and instead encourages reinvestment in the status quo. Further, it reinforces exclusionary social dynamics, which makes it difficult for many people to connect to Jewish community. This means increasing our emphasis on lay leadership, participatory philanthropy, representation—and the redefinition of clergy as specialized educators, counselors, spiritual guides, and chief empowerment officers. In turn, as more people feel empowered to harness their own Jewish tools and harvest their own Jewish wisdom, Judaism will become more central to their lives.

Seventh, we see a need for new spaces of spiritual community and communal organizations. Beyond mindset, people-centered purpose, and empowerment, we need to consider technology and the hybrid nature of in-person and online experiences for many people. Bringing rural, suburban, and urban centers of Judaism together will foster dynamism and opportunity and create new pathways of efficiency. We see the bloom of more digital-content creators who can scale spiritual, cultural, and educational offerings on a national level, while local lay and professional leaders can center on relationship-building and empowerment. This in turn may encourage the reimagining of both physical and virtual spaces and new ways of knitting these spaces together. Curation matters more in a time of unbounded choice, as does a renewed emphasis on authentic connection, deep learning, and a broader spectrum of spiritual practices and prayer experiences.

Finally, we see the need to awaken to new purpose. When we engage with our communal fears and traumas, inherited from those who came before us, we see that while they are very real, they need not define our path forward. A century ago, American Jews reached for access, affluence, and integration. Even as antisemitism remains an ongoing challenge, this core purpose was largely achieved, underscoring the vision and determination of those who came before us. Now, as American Jewry possesses greater influence, affluence, and acceptance than ever before in our history, a new purpose begins to emerge. Judaism may now bloom as a wisdom tradition, accessible to all, providing tools to meet the deepest needs of today. Through spiritual practices that elevate gratitude and hope, we may use ancient tools to help build behaviors that strengthen mind, body, and spirit in the contemporary world. Through Jewish learning, text, and ethics, we may bring new vocabulary and complexity to the ideological tribalism of today and help teach America ways of forging connections across difference and divide. Heeding Isaiah's call that God's house shall be one for all people,[4] American Judaism may meet the most pressing need of our age: creating a space of belonging, cultivating relationships, and helping people flourish through community.

Furthermore, we can welcome in tens of millions of people who are seeking a spiritual home but are disenfranchised by tenets or practices of their communities of origin. We cannot simply allow this opportunity to pass us by, but need to seize it and use our awakening to spark a revival in society that transcends political divides. America has largely embraced us, and now we have a corresponding duty to our adoptive homeland and second center of life.

We can awaken to the budding fruit, the fragrant vines, and the seedlings that have already begun to sprout. As our ancestors have done for millennia, we leave that which has been familiar in search of a new future. Many feelings naturally swirl at such a juncture. Above them all is a call of purpose, one that will not only enliven our Diaspora, but change the world around us as well. From the very beginning, with Eden behind us, we searched for a new place of promise. The nature and location of that land has changed in every era, even as its promise gave us continual purpose. It begins by hearing the call, both divine and human, and stepping forward in response.

Awaken, my dear one, my fair one, and go.

A Brief History of Jewish Awakenings

Our awakening is not only a Jewish opportunity, but an American tradition. It is a manifestation of new spiritual needs, unbounded possibilities, and individual empowerment.

Jewish history in the Americas[1] predates by two centuries the birth of the United States, while our patterns of community life can be traced to the 1830s, when German Jews began to arrive in meaningful numbers.[2] B'nai B'rith was founded in the 1840s; leading figures in what became the Reform movement began pushing for ritual reforms by the 1850s; military chaplains began to serve Jews in the 1860s; the Union of American Hebrew Congregations (now the Union for Reform Judaism) and Hebrew Union College were founded in the 1870s; and the first internal census by and of American Jews calculated a population of 250,000 by 1880.[3] Rising cohorts across proto-denominations reimagined the organs of Jewish community, learning, and leadership.

By the early 1880s, a combination of terrifying pogroms and advances in transportation began pushing hundreds of thousands of Jews out of Eastern Europe and enabling them to more readily voyage to the United States. Perhaps two million arrived by the start of World War I.[4]

While German Jews maintained positions of relative privilege and influence in American society, this burgeoning population of newer immigrants from Eastern Europe required new ways to articulate an identity that was at once Jewish and American, often based on a more traditional framework.

In 1898, more traditional practitioners founded the Union of Orthodox Jewish Congregations; in 1899, the growing Diaspora founded the National Conference of Jewish Charities; by 1900, Jewish labor activists founded the Workmen's Circle; and by 1901, the leaders of the Conservative movement founded the Rabbinical Assembly.[5]

Each organization represented a new vision for American Jews—a new approach to tradition, political engagement, philanthropy, or mutual aid. Each one sought to enable the Jewish community to make its way into mainstream American society while retaining key aspects of identity, values, and practice. Whether or not these organizations are still active today, they succeeded beyond their wildest dreams in transforming a community of disparate immigrants into a community of organized influencers.

Even so, American Jewry retained fears of ostracism, antisemitism, and total assimilation. The Diaspora and its organizations hold collective memories of the 1915 lynching of Leo Frank, the Ku Klux Klan, and "Jew hunts" of the 1940s.[6] They remember the exclusion of Jews from elite universities through a system of quotas and social barriers. They remember losing (or never receiving) deserved promotions. They remember the mantra of survival because of how hard it felt for our community to integrate and thrive.

World War II further entrenched in the Jewish psyche the mantra of struggle and survival. German fascism severed the artery of the Jewish heartland in Europe, destroying six million Jews—and perhaps 90 percent of Torah scholars,[7] much of the Yiddish language, and countless communities. Survival was no longer just the refrain of immigrants trying to make their way in the United States. For the first time in millennia, the entire Jewish people was at risk of destruction. Even the birth of the modern State of Israel in 1948 could not salve the wounds of our Diaspora. If the government in Germany, once home to the leading Jewish intellects and the most integrated Diaspora in the world, could murder so many souls, could America be next?

Historian Jonathan Sarna reflects that survival became so integral to the American Diaspora that it became essential to our story as a minority community: "Fear for the survival of Judaism in the United States served, as so often it would, as a potent stimulus for change."[8] Each stream of Judaism, and the leaders driving them, believed that theirs was the fight to safeguard Judaism's very survival. It inspired generations of Jews to dedicate time, talent, and treasure to the cause. It can still be seen within the ethos of collective responsibility that undergirds the Hebrew Free Loan Society, seminaries, colleges, local synagogues, federations, and professional associations. With fear of collapse and destruction real and tangible for both immigrant generations and those that bore witness from afar to the destruction of European Jewry, a desperation to survive brought out the greatness from within.

Central institutions bloomed alongside Jewish heroes, who helped model the strength of American Jews. Rabbis Abraham Joshua Heschel and Joseph Soloveitchik became intellectual exemplars of the American Diaspora. Major league baseball players Hank Greenberg and Sandy Koufax earned their places in the National Baseball Hall of Fame, while comedians Mel Brooks and Carl Reiner rose as stars on the screen. Celebrities like Sammy Davis Jr. and Marilyn Monroe chose to become Jewish. These exemplars illustrated different iterations of the ideal of a people, modeling how one could move from surviving as a minority community to thriving as one. They showed that Jewish access and power could grow on the national scene and strengthened the sense of success and stability shaped through Jewish institutions.

By the 1960s and 1970s, Jews began to ascend professional ranks in countless fields, even amid continued antisemitism and restrictions.[9] Even so, they did not feel secure. Denominations expanded into suburbia and around the country as an answer to the Holocaust and the decimation of European Jewry, showing that we could survive in America by virtue of our mighty institutions. American Jews redoubled their commitment to creating centers of Jewish life, making survival the call to religious revival. By 1960, more than 60 percent of American Jews were denominationally and institutionally affiliated.[10] It was a badge of honor, proof of our strength, and a way of finding others who shared similar experiences of grief, growth, and hope. When called to survive, we thrived.

In the succeeding decades, as Jews prospered and the specter of our Diaspora's destruction waned, the rallying cry lost its relevance and began to displace other calls to community. As our communal institutions continue to redouble the cry, they create distance between themselves and the American Jews they wish to serve.

Antisemitism metastasized in new and insidious ways, even as Jews became the best-liked religious group in the United States.[11] But our institutions focused only on antisemitic violence.[12] Intermarriage became the pervasive trend in American Jewish relationship, even as Jewish identity and Jewish pride grew. But our institutions focused on intermarriage.[13] Israel's excoriation by the international community deepened, even as Israel became an economic, social, and military power. But our institutions focused on advocacy and charity for a homeland that no longer needed our help.

The cry to survive now impedes our ability to thrive. Yet the growing gap between human need and institutional offering allows space for the awakening to take root and reconnect people in new ways, with greater clarity of purpose. The discomfort inherent in a period of spiritual awakening can prove productive, leading to institutional renewal and a renewed alignment of people and purpose. Rather than denigrating disaffiliation or shying away from difficult questions about ourselves as leaders, we would do well to study the underlying causes of communal ennui and disillusionment. Doing so will help us anticipate the scope and trajectory of the unfolding awakening and support its emergence.

Our awakening is not only a Jewish opportunity, but an American tradition. It is a symptom of new spiritual needs, unbounded possibilities, and individual empowerment. In the early nineteenth century, the Second Great Awakening burst forth for Protestant Christians,[14] as spiritual and communal yearning ignited across the United States. A new nation, with cries of personal freedom, unleashed a footrace for hearts, minds, and spirits. New modes of worship, new theologies, new leadership models, and new understandings of belonging adapted religion to the frontier of this new nation and life in once-unthinkable ways.[15]

State governments across the country eliminated subsidies to former religious monopolies from the colonial period,[16] permitting unfettered competition between traditions and practices. According to author Steven Waldman, in 1776, there were 65 Methodist churches in the entire country; by 1850, there were 13,302. In 1784, there were 471 Baptist churches; in 1848, there were 7,920.[17] The percentage of Americans who were affiliated with a house of worship doubled during this period.[18]

Rationalism and deism gave way to emotional forms of "revival" worship, inviting immediate conversion to Christianity.[19] Loose networks emerged by denomination and geography, but individual preachers—however formally trained—seized the opportunity to spread the gospel in ways still familiar in decentralized evangelical communities.

Social flux gave way to new formulations of belief and practice.[20] Though the surprising by-product of an American Revolution rooted in Enlightenment values, the Great Awakening was a means by which to test the boundaries of personal freedom. They answered human needs in a uniquely American way, as a response to rapid change. Historian William McLoughlin explains:

> Great awakenings (and the revivals that are a part of them) are the results, not of depressions, wars, or epidemics, but of critical disjunctions in our self-understanding. They are not brief outbursts of mass emotionalism by one group or another, but profound cultural transformations affecting all Americans and extending over a generation or more. Awakenings begin in periods of cultural distortion and grave personal stress, when we lose faith in the legitimacy of our norms, the viability of our institutions, and the authority of our leaders in church and state. They eventuate in basic restructurings of our institutions and redefinitions of our social goals.[21]

Today, we are living through another awakening, not only within the Jewish community, but also within American society as a whole. For the first time in a hundred years, the majority of Americans are unchurched,[22] while spiritual yearnings continue beyond the walls of institutions.[23] Nineteen percent of Americans say that they do not have a religious identity at all,[24] even as 63 percent of unaffiliated Americans believe in God.[25] Religion is not keeping pace with social change or the people it purports to serve.

Technology has led to the dramatic reshuffling of power in our society, giving some people vastly more wealth and influence than they ever could have imagined, while threatening to displace a multitude of jobs and workers. Its outgrowth into social media and platforms for commerce has reinforced "silos" and "echo chambers," increasing polarization and raising fundamental questions about the healthy bounds of free speech, the nature of community, and how much our online personas have come to serve as proxies of identity.[26]

It is difficult to find a community whose causes reflect such specific individual interests. The result is profound isolation as we pursue the elusive community that is in perfect alignment with our own views. Social isolationism and loneliness are now the twenty-first-century crisis, with increased mortality risk from persistent loneliness, comparable to that from smoking.[27]

We are free to learn, see, access, and experience nearly anything at any time for any reason. The human crisis before us stems from the dilemma of giving up seemingly limitless freedom in order to live ethically and to join collectively for our ethics to have an impact. Beyond the ephemera of material satisfaction and stimulation, we seek fulfillment through a higher purpose, deep relationships, and social justice. Like the Americans who experienced what felt like unbounded freedom in their nascent country, those blessed to have their material needs met experience a freedom that is even vaster and more complicated.[28]

In the framework of the philosopher Isaiah Berlin, there are positive and negative liberties—roughly speaking, the *freedom from* and the *freedom to*.[29] Technology has massively expanded our positive freedoms, though sometimes by increasing the negative ones. Our liberty to say whatever we want can keep others from being heard or make for cyberbullying. Our liberty to access any content we want can incentivize the mistreatment of people who are the subjects or objects of that same content—for example, in the case of pornography, "hit piece" articles verging on defamation, the unauthorized sharing of personal information through "doxing,"[30] and political polemics.

Jewish spiritual frameworks, by contrast, focus on negative freedoms: the freedom not to be defamed; the freedom not to experience objectification, sexualization, or the incitement of violence against you. As such, the Jewish awakening has been sparked by boundless positive freedoms, which prompt us to consider the negative freedoms we have lost and the social frameworks that we need to reclaim them.

Jewish tradition and practice are well positioned to help people navigate this time of change, complexity, uncertainty, and counter-productiveness of choice.[31] They provide age-old wisdom and a methodology of loving argumentation to navigate new situations with nuance. They encourage humility and mutual responsibility and open us to wonder about eternal questions of belief, humanity, and the cosmos.

Deeper inquiry into the Jewish awakening requires us to hold many realities in tension, notably concerning power and vulnerability, uniqueness and universality, intra-section and intersection, historical gleanings and emergent purpose. American Jews are socially integrated and outright embraced, while also bearing the weight of inherited trauma about antisemitism and ongoing vulnerability to hate crimes. We stand armored against the bigotry and barriers we face, while prioritizing the calls and causes of other marginalized identities in America. We are siloed by denomination and institution, even as new networks bloom across traditional lines and factionalism demands a response in the form of pluralism.[32] We question the loyalty of our own members, while teeming with new approaches to Jewish wisdom that could one day engage millions of Americans in Jewish practice.

Amid this dynamism and productive tension, we can center Jewish tradition in the spiritual awakening emerging before us. Realizing the full potential of this pivotal time will require innovation, reflection, experimentation, emotional support, and faith in the future. It will entail the continued assimilation of people with Jewish ancestry who do not feel that it plays a meaningful role in their lives. It will mean the articulation of Jewish practices and principles with newfound confidence and vulnerability. It will push us to move beyond a singular focus on peoplehood, all the while strengthening individuals and living out our purpose as a source of enlightenment and inspiration to the world. It will mean wading into the reality of multiple belongings and the complexity of identities that are Jewishly inspired. It will mean acknowledging the extent to which our Diaspora has succeeded beyond the wildest dreams of the first Jews to grace America's shores or the grassroots leaders who shaped our last awakening in the late nineteenth and early twentieth centuries. It will mean finding higher purpose and new goals to pursue. It will entail acknowledging the feelings of fracture and loss and entering this era of Jewish awakening with intention.

Judaism holds space for those questioning the existence of a Higher Power—and questioning so much about human life. It gives permission to wonder and inquire about belief and enables individuals to hone their ethical reasoning through a time-tested framework of associative logic, story, and human experience. Our tradition can help us uncover healthy bounds to otherwise limitless freedom—to sublimate norms for our actions from the ether of human experience.

If Americans are suffering from a lack of communal connection, spiritual practice, and the chance to ask eternal questions, it is little wonder that Introduction to Judaism and conversion classes are filled to capacity.[33] Jewish practices and ideas answer the needs of America's polity more than ever before. They speak not in a single voice, but in interwoven dialogues across centuries, which offer core ideas while leaving space for each individual to be heard. The sense of its time-honored "authenticity" adds to its allure, while the prominence of American Jews concretizes the value of living a Jewishly inspired life.

Many of our institutions find themselves lamentably ill-prepared to welcome in the spiritually homeless.[34] We have so fortified ourselves against intruders that we keep far too many people out. We question the motives of potential converts, demean those who dabble in our teachings, mock prayerful mispronunciations, normalize Ashkenazi skin tones, and ask people why they really would want to live Jewishly at all. We demand that newcomers proclaim their loyalty to the Jewish people before they understand what either "Jewish" or "people" might really mean to them or have the chance to explore Judaism without pressure or expectation.

In this age of fracture and fragmentation, Americans, and American Jews in particular, crave new ideas and threads of coherence. If other eras relied on ethnic identity or genetics, geography or economics, rising generations now call for new modes of connectivity. In turn, American Jews need a new story—one with greater complexity and tropes of prior transformations that inform those before us and provide affirmation for new ways to belong. The new Jewish awakening before us could help germinate an American awakening as well, lifting ancient technologies of wisdom and community for all.

This book expands once more our inherited American Jewish story, affirming the work of past dreamers and acknowledging that so many present failings are a function of their success. We look back on the purposes that drove prior generations toward the future and feel today the call to dream anew. We see and welcome the bloom of a Jewish awakening.

Afterword

The light bulb first went on while I was reading Rodger Kamenetz's *The Jew in the Lotus*, a book about the meeting between a diverse group of rabbis and His Holiness the Dalai Lama. As I read through the details of their wide-ranging discussion, touching on subjects from maintaining a community in Diaspora to passing a tradition down through the generations, I had a simple but powerful realization: *religions can learn from one another.*

That idea has guided virtually everything I've done in the field of religion ever since, from my doctoral dissertation on how Ismaili Muslims (my faith community) adapted to modernity, to my work now as founder and president of Interfaith Youth Core (IFYC), building an America that embraces all of its religious diversity.

That light bulb is shining brighter after reading *Awakenings* by Rabbis Joshua Stanton and Benjamin Spratt. Its purpose is to frame the dynamics faced by American Jews and chart a path to the thriving of their own particular community. But because the book does its work so well, I believe it effectively serves as a window into the challenges and opportunities that face American religion as a whole.

"We see the challenge to former structures of religious belonging and optimism for the dynamism seen throughout American Judaism," write Stanton and Spratt. That observation is just as relevant to communities ranging from American Buddhists to Unitarian Universalists. Everywhere the old forms seem to be breaking down, but people still yearn to be connected to community, divinity, and history.

Stanton and Spratt suggest that we embrace this energy, turn it into entrepreneurship, and create new forms. No matter how many stories we read about decline in religion, we should remind ourselves of the words that are emblazoned on the Jewish Theological Seminary: "The bush was not consumed." Reality has outpaced our organizational maps. No problem. People the world over from time immemorial have simply created new maps.

I love that Rabbis Stanton and Spratt offer Jewish history as a guide, telling the story of how Rabbi Akiva did not mourn when he saw the ruins of the Temple but rather was delighted. "We always knew these stones must come down. In order to move forward, this had to fall apart first. Now we can begin."

All of our religions have history and theology like this. I think about the emergence of everything from Catholic orders to Sufi tariqas—renewal movements that changed the map of entire religions.

We are at that point again. Rabbis Stanton and Spratt propose that we meet the moment with the generosity and power that are at the heart of all our religions. Their work gives me confidence that we can. As they write, "Our awakening is not only a Jewish opportunity, but an American tradition. It is a symptom of new spiritual needs [and] unbounded possibilities."

Dr. Eboo Patel
Founder and President of Interfaith Youth Core

Notes

Introduction

1   Solomon Schechter, *Inaugural Address*, Delivered November 20, 1902 (New York, 1903), 33, https://loc.gov/item/ltf90007565/.

2   "2021 AJS Institutional Members," Association for Jewish Studies, https://www.associationforjewishstudies.org/membership/current-ims.

3   Mordecai Besser, *A Census of Jewish Day Schools in the United States 2018–2019* (New York: AVI CHAI Foundation, 2020), 9, https://avichai.org/wp-content/uploads/2019/11/AVI-CHAI-Census-2018-2019-v3.pdf.

4   "1990 National Jewish Population Survey (NJPS 1990)," Berman Jewish Databank, https://www.jewishdatabank.org/databank/search-results/study/885. Over 50 percent of Jews were marrying someone who was not Jewish. For a helpful critique of the survey, see Sidney Goldstein, "Profile of American Jewry: Insights from the 1990 National Jewish Population Survey," *American Jewish Yearbook*, January 1, 1992, https://www.bjpa.org/search-results/publication/900.

5   Leslie Fiedler, *Fiedler on the Roof: Essays on Literature and Jewish Identity* (Boston: Godine, 1991), quoted in Goldstein, "Profile of American Jewry," 77. See also review of *Fiedler on the Roof*, by Leslie Fiedler, *Kirkus Reviews*, March 15, 1991, https://www.kirkusreviews.com/book-reviews/leslie-fiedler/fiedler-on-the-roof/.

6   "Jewish Continuity: The Next Generation," Pluralism Project at Harvard University, 2020, https://pluralism.org/files/pluralism/files/jewish_continuity-_the_next_generation.pdf.

7   Helene Berger, Linda Cornell Weinstein, and David G. Sacks, *Symposium on Intermarriage and Jewish Continuity* (New York: Council of Jewish Federations, 1991), https://www.bjpa.org/content/upload/bjpa/symp/SYMPOSIUM%20ON%20INTERMARRIAGE%20&%20JEWISH%20CONTINUITY%20VOL%20I%201991.pdf.

8   Gal Beckerman, "American Jews Face a Choice: Create Meaning or Fade Away," review of *The Chosen Wars: How Judaism Became an American Religion*, by Steven Weisman, *The New American Judaism: How Jews Practice Their Religion Today*, by Jack Wertheimer, *The Jewish American Paradox: Embracing Choice in a Changing World*, by Robert Mnookin, *God Is in the Crowd: Twenty-First Century Judaism*, by Tal Keinan, *Dear Zealots: Letters from a Divided Land*, by Amoz Oz, *New York Times*, November 12, 2018, https://www.nytimes.com/2018/11/12/books/review/steven-weisman-chosen-wars.html.

9   Israel Harel, "Assimilation Is the Failure of American Jewry, Not Israel," *Haaretz*, March 23, 2018, https://www.haaretz.com/opinion/assimilation-u-s-jewry-s-failure-1.5936970.

10   Erica Chernofsky, "The Jewish Fear of Intermarriage," *BBC News*, February 7, 2014, https://www.bbc.com/news/magazine-26067980.

11   Zack Beauchamp, "Israeli Minister Says US Jews Marrying Non-Jews Is 'Like a Second Holocaust,'" Vox, July 10, 2019, https://www.vox.com/2019/7/10/20687946/israel-minister-second-holocaust-intermarriage.

12   Alan Dershowitz, *The Vanishing American Jew* (New York: Simon and Schuster, 1998), 1.

13   "Jewish Continuity: The Next Generation."

14   Jonathan Sarna, *American Judaism* (New Haven, CT: Yale University Press, 2004), 373–74.

15   Data derives from "1990 National Jewish Population Survey (NJPS)," Berman Jewish DataBank, https://www.jewishdatabank.org/databank/search-results?search=1990+njps; and Pew Research Center, *Jewish Americans* in 2020 (Washington, DC: Pew Research Center, May 11, 2021), https://www.pewforum.org/2021/05/11/jewish-americans-in-2020/.

16   Ninety-four percent of Jews are "proud to be Jewish," according to the 2013 *A Portrait of Jewish Americans* by the Pew Research Center, https://www.pewforum.org/2013/10/01/jewish-american-beliefs-attitudes-culture-survey/; and 75 percent say that they have a "strong sense of belonging." We first learned of this disconnect during a Rabbis Without Borders retreat, led by Rabbi Rebecca Sirbu, then of Clal—The National Jewish Center for Learning and Leadership.

17   We are grateful to Dr. Jack Wertheimer of the Jewish Theological Seminary for his time and support of this book project and recommend his award-winning book *New American Judaism* (Princeton, NJ: Princeton University Press, 2018) for those interested in another framing of current trends.

18   One might aptly argue that the modern State of Israel could likewise become a victim of its own successes and fall to its own might.

19   Masood Farivar, "Survey: 63% of US Jews Encountered Antisemitism over Last 5 Years," Voice of America, March 13, 2021, https://www.voanews.com/usa/survey-63-us-jews-encountered-antisemitism-over-last-5-years.

20   Pew Research Center, "Feelings toward Religious Groups," in *What Americans Know about Religion* (Washington, DC: Pew Research Center, July 23, 2019), https://www.pewforum.org/2019/07/23/feelings-toward-religious-groups/. See also earlier Pew Research Center reports: "How Americans Feel about Religious Groups," July 16, 2014, https://www.pewforum.org/2014/07/16/how-americans-feel-about-religious-groups/; and "Americans Express Increasingly Warm Feelings toward Religious Groups," February 15, 2017, https://www.pewforum.org/2017/02/15/americans-express-increasingly-warm-feelings-toward-religious-groups/.

21   Ari Kelman, Aaron Hahn Tapper, Izabel Fonseca, and Aliya Saperstein, "Counting Inconsistencies: An Analysis of American Jewish Population Studies, with a Focus on Jews of Color" (University of San Francisco, May 2019), https://www.jewishdatabank.org/content/upload/bjdb/2019_Counting_Inconsistencies_Methodological_Appendix_Focus_on_Jews_of_Color.pdf.

22   Pew Research Center, *Jewish Americans* in 2020.

23   While factionalism is on the rise, the ethic of intra-religious pluralism can bring Jews together across divides.

24   This is drawn from our interview with Nigel Savage on February 10, 2021.

25   This is based upon our interview with Rabbi Elan Babchuk on January 12, 2021.

26   Jonathan Sarna, *A Great Awakening: The Transformation That Shaped Twentieth Century American Judaism and Its Implications for Today* (New York: Council for Initiatives in Jewish Education, 1995), https://www.brandeis.edu/hornstein/sarna/americanjewishcultureandscholarship/A-Great-Awakening_Jonathan-D.-Sarna_1995.pdf. Sarna deserves credit for inspiring us to look upon the present era as another Jewish awakening—in the classical and historical sense. We are profoundly grateful.

27   Pew Research Center, *Jewish Americans* in 2020. Professor Jonathan Sarna has also helped us reflect on the extent to which this narrative pervades non-Orthodox circles of Jewish life and no longer is central to ultra-Orthodox and Modern Orthodox groups. Sarna cites the statistic that one in three Jewish children under the age of five is Orthodox (conveyed via email, October 7, 2021).

28   For more on this, we recommend the studies and reports of the Public Religion Research Institute, as well as the publications of Dr. Robert P. Jones.

29   Michael Lipka and Claire Gecewicz, "More Americans Now Say They're Spiritual but Not Religious," Pew Research Center, September 6, 2017, https://www.pewresearch.org/fact-tank/2017/09/06/more-americans-now-say-theyre-spiritual-but-not-religious/.

30   "The Jewish Emergent Network comprises the leaders of seven pathbreaking Jewish communities from across the United States who have come together in the spirit of collaboration. These include: IKAR in Los Angeles, Kavana in Seattle, The Kitchen in San Francisco, Mishkan in Chicago, Sixth & I in Washington, DC, and Lab/Shul and Romemu in New York." For more, see Jewish Emergent Network, http://www.jewishemergentnetwork.org/.

31   See, for example, the establishment of the learning centers in Lakewood, New Jersey, eight decades ago. They continue to grow and thrive. David Landes, "How Lakewood, N.J., Is Redefining What It Means to Be Orthodox in America," *Tablet*, June 5, 2013, https://www.tabletmag.com/sections/community/articles/lakewood-redefining-orthodoxy.

32   This comes from an interview that we conducted with Rabbi Leon Morris.

33   Michael L. Satlow, "Defining Judaism: Accounting for 'Religions' in the Study of Religion," *Journal of the American Academy of Religion* 74, no. 4 (2006): 837–60, http://www.jstor.org/stable/4139954.

34   Exodus 3:2, New Jewish Publication Society translation, from *JPS Hebrew-English Tanakh* (Philadelphia: Jewish Publication Society, 1999).

Chapter 1

1   Numbers 20:4, New Jewish Publication Society translation.

2   Betsy Cooper, Daniel Cox, Rachel Lienesch, and Robert P. Jones, "The Divide Over America's Future: 1950 or 2050? Findings from the 2016 American Values Survey," PRRI, October 25, 2016, https://www.prri.org/research/poll-1950s-2050-divided-nations-direction-post-election/.

3   Taylor A. FioRito and Clay Routledge, "Is Nostalgia a Past or Future-Oriented Experience? Affective, Behavioral, Social Cognitive, and Neuroscientific Evidence," *Frontiers in Psychology*, June 3, 2020, https://www.frontiersin.org/articles/10.3389/fpsyg.2020.01133/full.

4   Edoardo Campanella and Marta Dassù, *Anglo Nostalgia: The Politics of Emotion in a Fractured West* (London: Hurst, 2019), 1.

5   Arnold M. Eisen, *Rethinking Modern Judaism: Ritual, Commandment, Community* (Chicago: University of Chicago Press, 1999), 181.

6   Noah Bernamoff and Rae Bernamoff, *The Mile End Cookbook: Redefining Jewish Comfort Food, from Hash to Hamantaschen* (New York: Clarkson Potter, 2012), 14.

7   The evocative words sung three times on the eve of Yom Kippur.

8   Prayerful guidebook to the Passover seder, which literally means "the telling."

9   Barbara Kirshenblatt-Gimblett, "Food and Drink," *YIVO Encyclopedia of Jews in Eastern Europe*, 2011, https://yivoencyclopedia.org/article.aspx/food_and_drink.

10   Israel Goldschmidt, "The Jewish Cantor in History—or—Music in Medieval Judaism," *Journal of Synagogue Music 44*, no. 1 (September 2019): 4–13, https://www.cantors.org/wp-content/uploads/2019/08/919-Compressed.pdf.

11   Joshua Rothenberg, "Demythologizing the Shtetl," *Midstream*, March 1981: 25–31.

12   James Nevius, "The Rise and Fall of New York City's Private Social Clubs," Curbed New York, June 17, 2015, https://ny.curbed.com/2015/6/17/9950758/the-rise-and-fall-of-new-york-citys-private-social-clubs.

13   Hadas Binyamini, "Philanthropy and the 'Jewish Continuity Crisis,'" Public Books, April 6, 2021, https://www.publicbooks.org/philanthropy-and-the-jewish-continuity-crisis/.

14   Matt Lebovic, "When American Jews Described Their Own Intermarriage as a 'Second Holocaust,'" Times of Israel, July 12, 2019, https://www.timesofisrael.com/when-american-jews-described-their-own-intermarriage-as-a-second-holocaust/.

15   Abraham Joshua Heschel, *Thunder in the Soul: To Be Known by God*, ed. Robert Erlewine (Walden, NY: Plough, 2021), 3.

16   Noah Phillips, "All Eyes Are on Jon Ossoff," *Moment*, August 14, 2019, https://moment-mag.com/all-eyes-are-on-jon-ossoff/.

Chapter 2

1   Richard Handler and Jocelyn Linnekin, "Tradition, Genuine or Spurious," *Journal of American Folklore* 97, no. 385 (1984): 273–90.

2   Zvi Ron, "The Origin and Development of the Custom for the Bride to Circle the Groom Three or Seven Times," *Zutot* 17, no. 1 (2019): 1–14, https://doi.org/10.1163/18750214-12171084. To clarify, the tradition is centuries, not millennia, old. By the standards of Jewish history, this makes it a relative newcomer.

3   Olga Goldberg-Mulkiewicz, "Dress," *YIVO Encyclopedia of Jews in Eastern Europe*, 2010, https://yivoencyclopedia.org/article.aspx/Dress.

4   Kol Nidrei, a prayer repeated three times, emphasizes the annulment of oaths. It is likely linked to Conversos—Jews posing as Catholics during and after the Spanish Inquisition.

5   Shiva.com, https://www.shiva.com.

6   Kabalatalism.com, https://www.kabalatalisman.com.

7   As captured astutely by Stuart Charmé, "A position can be authentically Jewish only by realizing its own potential inauthenticity: that it is historical, may be given different meanings at different moments in history, and becomes fixed or congealed only at the price of bad faith." Stuart Z. Charmé, "Varieties of Authenticity in Contemporary Jewish Identity," *Jewish Social Studies*, n.s., 6, no. 2 (2000): 158.

8   Lawrence A. Hoffman, ed., *My People's Prayer Book*, vol. 8, *Kabbalat Shabbat* (Woodstock, VT: Jewish Lights, 1997), 20.

9   Jane Eisner, "The Embarrassing Pay Gap in the Board Rooms of Jewish Not-for-Profits," *Forward*, December 12, 2017, https://forward.com/opinion/389778/the-embarrassing-pay-gap-in-the-board-rooms-of-jewish-not-for-profits/.

10   Leading Edge, *The Gender Gap in Jewish Nonprofit Leadership: An Ecosystem View*, August 18, 2021, https://leading-edge.cdn.prismic.io/leading-edge/aacd0b8e-5a8a-4c4b-b62a-d0ae6dd3333e_The+Gender+Gap+in+Jewish+Nonprofit+Leadership+—+An+Ecosystem+View-2021-10-21.pdf.

11   "About," Reform Pay Equity Initiative, March 5, 2020, https://reformpayequity.org/about/.

12   Brian Palmer, "What Type of Clergy Get the Highest Salaries?," Slate, January 12, 2012, https://slate.com/news-and-politics/2012/01/how-much-do-rabbis-priests-pastors-and-imams-earn.html.

13   Numbers 11:29, New Jewish Publication Society translation.

Chapter 3

1   Gary Baum, "Hollywood's Hottest $150 Million Project Is an 83-Year-Old Synagogue," *Hollywood Reporter*, May 30, 2012, https://www.hollywoodreporter.com/movies/movie-news/hollywood-jewish-wilshire-boulevard-temple-renovation-150-million-330471/.

2   Marc Margolius, Alan Divack, and Ben Greenberg, "Tackling Your Synagogue's Biggest Financial Challenge," eJewish Philanthropy, February 22, 2016, https://ejewishphilanthropy.com/tackling-your-synagogues-biggest-financial-challenge/.

Chapter 4

1   The authors are also cofounders of Tribe.

2   Uriel Heilman, "Who's Leading the U.S. Rabbinical School Scene?," Jewish Telegraphic Agency, September 26, 2017, https://www.jta.org/2014/03/18/united-states/whos-leading-the-u-s-rabbinical-school-scene.

3   Josh Nathan-Kazis, "Where Are All the Non-Orthodox Rabbis?," *Forward*, February 18, 2015, https://forward.com/news/214663/where-are-all-the-non-orthodox-rabbis/.

4   Some, like the Modern Orthodox seminary at Yeshiva University, attempt to keep enrollment numbers up by eliminating costs for rabbinical students. Even these tactics of subsidizing costs failed to stem the decline.

5   Hayim Herring and Jason Miller, "Adding Context to the Diminishing Rabbinical School Enrollment Numbers," Hayim Herring—Rabbi, Entrepreneur, Consultant, February 25, 2015, https://hayimherring.com/adding-context-diminishing-rabbinical-school-enrollment-numbers/.

6   Josh Nathan-Kazis, "On the Pulpit, Rabbis Earn More Than Christian Clergy," *Forward*, September 15, 2010, https://forward.com/news/131325/on-the-pulpit-rabbis-earn-more-than-christian-cler/.

7   Brian Palmer, "What Type of Clergy Get the Highest Salaries?," Slate, January 12, 2012, https://slate.com/news-and-politics/2012/01/how-much-do-rabbis-priests-pastors-and-imams-earn.html.

8   Ibid.

9   Steven Davidson, "How Much Do Top Jewish Non-Profit Leaders Make?," *Forward*, December 11, 2017, https://forward.com/news/388240/how-much-do-top-jewish-non-profit-leaders-make/.

10 This is found in the code of ethics for the rabbinic unions of the Reconstructionist, Reform, Conservative, and Orthodox movements. For more, see "Reconstructionist Rabbinical Association Code of Ethics," April 2016, "XIV: "Relationships among Organizations and Congregation, Rabbis and Other Professionals," https://therra.org/Ethics%20Code%202016.pdf; "Central Conference of American Rabbis Code of Ethics," 2021, "II: Rabbinic Relationships," https://www.ccarnet.org/about-us/ccar-ethics/; "Rabbinic Assembly: A Code of Professional Conduct," October 2018, "IV: Relationship between Rabbis," https://www.rabbinicalassembly.org/sites/default/files/public/ethical_guidelines/code-of-conduct-2018-members.pdf; Rabbinical Council of America, "Code of Conduct," April 2018, "XIII: Rabbinic Relationships, B.1," https://rabbis.org/pdfs/Code_of_Conduct_3_13_2018.pdf.

11 These include Rabbi Rick Jacobs (URJ), Rabbi Jacob Blumenthal (USCJ), Rabbi Deborah Waxman (Reconstructing Judaism), and Rabbi Josh Joseph (OU). Of significance, currently both the chancellor of the Jewish Theological Seminary of America and the head of Hebrew Union College–Jewish Institute of Religion are scholars and laypeople. This might portend further steps toward lay leadership across denominations and institutions.

12 "Union for Reform Judaism and Consolidated Entities: Consolidated Financial Statements for Years Ended December, 31 2020 and 2019," 12, https://urj.org/sites/default/files/2021-10/Union-for-Reform-Judaism-and-Consolidated-Entities-12.31.20.pdf.

13 This phenomenon is paralleled in other denominations.

14 Gary Rosenblatt, "Scarsdale Rabbi to Lead Reform," *Jewish Week,* March 22, 2011, https://jewishweek.timesofisrael.com/scarsdale-rabbi-to-lead-reform/.

15 Jay Ruderman, "Time for a Change: How Our Major Jewish Organizations Can Better Represent the Diversity of Our American Jewish Community," *The Blogs,* Times of Israel, May 24, 2018, https://blogs.timesofisrael.com/time-for-a-change-how-our-major-jewish-organizations-can-better-represent-the-diversity-of-our-american-jewish-community/.

16 William Barrett, "America's Top Charities 2020," *Forbes,* December 11, 2020, https://www.forbes.com/lists/top-charities/#749f708b5f50.

17 Lila Corwan Berman and Matthew Berkman, "Democratizing American Jewish Philanthropy: New Models for Capital Circulation," NYU Applied Research Collective for American Jewry, 2019, https://static1.squarespace.com/static/56abab9d8b38d4b28f7d183e/t/5e139d721db9945228788173/1578343795532/LC-DemocratizingAJP_121219.pdf.

18 "AJC 2019 Survey of American Jewish Opinion," American Jewish Committee, June 2, 2019, https://www.ajc.org/news/survey2019. Sixty-four percent of American Jews support a two-state solution to the Israeli-Palestinian conflict.

Chapter 5

1 Numbers 22:2–25:9.

2 Numbers 24:5–6, adapted from the New Jewish Publication Society translation.

3 Robert D. Putnam and David E. Campbell, *American Grace: How Religion Divides and Unites Us* (New York: Simon and Schuster, 2010), 153. For more see: https://tannerlectures.utah.edu/_resources/documents/a-to-z/p/Putnam_10.pdf.

4 Pew Research Center, *What Americans Know about Religion* (Washington, DC: Pew Research Center, July 23, 2019, https://www.pewforum.org/2019/07/23/feelings-toward-religious-groups/; Michael Lipka, "U.S. Jews Know a Lot about Religion—But Other Americans Know Little about Judaism," Pew Research Center, August 18, 2020, https://www.pewresearch.org/fact-tank/2019/08/01/u-s-jews-know-a-lot-about-religion-but-other-americans-know-little-about-judaism/; Ben Sales, "Study: Americans Don't Know Much about Jews, but Love Them Anyway," Times of Israel, July 23, 2019, https://www.timesofisrael.com/study-americans-dont-know-much-about-jews-but-love-them-anyway/; and Ben Sales, "Americans Love Jews but Are Clueless about Judaism, Survey Finds," *Forward,* July 24, 2019, https://forward.com/fast-forward/428144/americans-don-t-know-much-about-judaism-but-love-the-jews-survey-says/.

5 For more on Jewish writers: "On Being Jewish, American and a Writer," *New York Times,* October 2, 2017, www.nytimes.com/2017/10/02/t-magazine/jewish-american-novelists.html.

6 Jennifer Greenberg, "Hold the Phone! Pink Is Jewish!?," Time Out Israel, January 11, 2017, https://www.timeout.com/israel/music/hold-the-phone-pink-is-jewish.

7 Becka A. Alper and Alan Cooperman, "10 Key Findings about Jewish Americans," Pew Research Center, May 11, 2021, https://www.pewresearch.org/fact-tank/2021/05/11/10-key-findings-about-jewish-americans/.

8   Mark Oppenheimer, "Surprising Trends Driving Conversion to Judaism," *Tablet*, May 13, 2021, https://www.tabletmag.com/sections/community/articles/conversion-not-just-for-marriage-anymore.

9   Nathan Glazer, *We Are All Multiculturalists Now* (Cambridge, MA: Harvard University Press, 2003).

10   Pew Research Center, "Marriage, Families, and Children," chapter 4 in *Jewish Americans in 2020* (Washington, DC: Pew Research Center, May 11, 2021), https://www.pewforum.org/2021/05/11/marriage-families-and-children/.

11   Theodore Sasson et al., "Millennial Children of Intermarriage: Religious Upbringing, Identification, and Behavior among Children of Jewish and Non-Jewish Parents," *Contemporary Jewry* 37, no. 1 (2017): 99–123.

12   Pew Research Center, "Marriage, Families, and Children," https://www.pewforum.org/2021/05/11/marriage-families-and-children/.

13   Lydia Kukoff, "Choosing Judaism, Redux," *Sh'ma* 39/654 (November 2008): 1, https://www.bjpa.org/content/upload/bjpa/nov0/nov08kukoff.pdf.

14   Rick Jacobs, "As Numerous as the Stars of Heaven," Union for Reform Judaism, December 14, 2020, https://urj.org/blog/numerous-stars-heaven.

15   "Kitchen Careers: The Shiksa in the Kitchen, Food Blogger," PBS Food, September 1, 2011, https://www.pbs.org/food/features/kitchen-careers-the-shiksa-in-the-kitchen/.

16   Mark Oppenheimer, Stephanie Butnick, and Liel Leibovitz, "The Conversion Episode, 2020," *Unorthodox* (podcast), episode 230, *Tablet*, May 27, 2020, https://www.tabletmag.com/podcasts/unorthodox/episode-230-jewish-conversion-stories-shavuot.

17   Lebo Diseko, "Tiffany Haddish's Black Mitzvah and Her Journey of Jewish Discovery," *BBC News*, December 16, 2019, https://www.bbc.com/news/world-africa-50686266.

18   Angela W. Buchdahl, "Kimchee on the Seder Plate," Facing History and Ourselves, June 1, 2003, https://www.facinghistory.org/resource-library/kimchee-seder-plate.

19   Tova Ricardo, "Grants on the Ground: A Steppingstone towards More JoC Religious Leaders: Jews of Color Initiative," Jews of Color Initiative, Tides Center, December 3, 2020, https://jewsofcolorinitiative.org/grants-on-the-ground-a-steppingstone-towards-more-joc-religious-leaders/.

20   Marc D. Angel and Avi Weiss, "Thou Shalt Not Oppress the Convert," Times of Israel, November 22, 2016, https://www.timesofisrael.com/thou-shalt-not-oppress-the-convert/; and Menachem Posner, "18 Amazing Converts to Judaism You Should Know," Chabad, https://www.chabad.org/library/article_cdo/aid/4098800/jewish/18-Amazing-Converts-to-Judaism-You-Should-Know.htm.

21   Aaron Potek, "Rabbi Rant: Intermarriage Isn't Good, or Bad," GatherDC, July 19, 2017, https://gatherdc.org/2017/06/21/intermarriage-isnt-good-or-bad/.

22   Aish HaTorah also is worthy of mention as a remarkably effective, visible in-reach organization that spans the globe.

23   Ron Csillag, "The Secrets of Chabad's Global Expansion," Canadian Jewish News, May 28, 2018, https://www.cjnews.com/living-jewish/the-secrets-of-chabads-global-expansion.

24   Rena Udkoff, "Ideal Partnerships for an Ideal Cause," Chabad Lubavitch World Headquarters News, January 9, 2020, http://www2.lubavitch.com/news/article/2109299/Ideal-Partnerships-For-An-Ideal-Cause.html.

25 Pew Research Center, *Jewish Americans in 2020* (Washington, DC: Pew Research Center, May 14, 2021), https://www.pewforum.org/2021/05/11/jewish-americans-in-2020/.

26 Multiple Chabad rabbis use this turn of phrase when embracing Jews by Choice.

27 For more, see Joseph Telushkin, *The Rebbe: The Life and Teachings of Menachem M. Schneerson* (New York: HarperCollins, 2014).

28 Menachem M. Schneerson, "The House Is on Fire, and Our Children Are Inside," The Rebbe, Chabad, 1964, https://www.chabad.org/therebbe/letters/default_cdo/aid/1264/jewish/The-House-Is-on-Fire-and-Our-Children-Are-Inside.htm.

Chapter 6

1   Pew Research Center, "The Religious Composition of the 117th Congress," Pew Research Center, January 4, 2021, https://www.pewforum.org/2021/01/04/faith-on-the-hill-2021/; and Pew Research Center, *Jewish Americans in 2020* (Washington, DC: Pew Research Center, May 14, 2021), https://www.pewforum.org/2021/05/11/jewish-americans-in-2020/.

2   Marc J. Perry, "Looking Back at the Remarkable History of the Nobel Prize from 1901–2019 Using Maps, Charts and Tables," American Enterprise Institute (AEI), October 14, 2019, https://www.aei.org/carpe-diem/looking-back-at-the-remarkable-history-of-the-nobel-prize-from-1901-2019-using-maps-charts-and-tables/.

3   TOI staff, "5 Jews Make Forbes' List of Top 10 Wealthiest Americans," Times of Israel, October 6, 2018, https://www.timesofisrael.com/5-jews-make-forbes-list-of-top-10-wealthiest-americans/.

4   Uriel Heilman, "Biden, Harris and Their Families Are Making Jewish History on Inauguration Day," Times of Israel, January 20, 2021, https://www.timesofisrael.com/biden-harris-and-their-families-are-making-jewish-history-on-inauguration-day/; and Jacob Kornbluh, "Yiddish Professor Goes Viral in Town Hall with President Biden" *Forward*, February 17, 2021, https://forward.com/news/464270/yiddish-professor-goes-viral-in-town-hall-with-president-biden/.

5   "Doors of Ivy League Colleges Reported Wide Open for Jewish Students," Jewish Telegraphic Agency, April 18, 1967, https://www.jta.org/1967/04/18/archive/doors-of-ivy-league-colleges-reported-wide-open-for-jewish-students.

6   Maristella Mbotticini and Zvi Eckstein, "The Chosen Few: A New Explanation of Jewish Success," *PBS New Hour*, April 18, 2013, https://www.pbs.org/newshour/economy/the-chosen-few-a-new-explanati.

7   Pew Research Center, "Sharp Rise in the Share of Americans Saying Jews Face Discrimination," Pew Research Center, April 15, 2019, https://www.pewresearch.org/politics/2019/04/15/sharp-rise-in-the-share-of-americans-saying-jews-face-discrimination/; and "ADL Calls for Improved Hate Crime Reporting in Response to New FBI Data," Anti-Defamation League, November 16, 2020, https://www.adl.org/news/press-releases/adl-calls-for-improved-hate-crime-reporting-in-response-to-new-fbi-data.

8   Pew Research Center, "Antisemitism and Jewish Views on Discrimination," chapter 6 in *Jewish Americans in 2020* (Washington, DC: Pew Research Center, May 11, 2021), https://www.pewforum.org/2021/05/11/antisemitism-and-jewish-views-on-discrimination/.

9   Julie Bykowicz and Natalie Andrews, "Pro-Israel Group Lobbies for U.S. Aid, Funds Congressional Trips," *Wall Street Journal*, February 14, 2019, https://www.wsj.com/articles/pro-israel-group-lobbies-for-u-s-aid-funds-congressional-trips-11550174834.

10 We are using the best publicly available data on these two august organizations. "2019 Consolidated Financial Information," Anti-Defamation League, https://www.adl.org/media/15406/download; the $110 million figure includes $81 million in operating revenues plus endowment fund contributions and other restricted contributions. KPMG, LLP, "American Jewish Committee and Affiliates Consolidated Financial Statements and Schedule," American Jewish Committee, December 31, 2018, https://www.ajc.org/sites/default/files/pdf/2019-07/American%20Jewish%20Committee%20and%20Affiliates%2012-31-18%20FINAL%20%287.24.2019%29%20-%20Daniel%20Goldwater_0.pdf.

11 Steven Windmueller, "American Jewish Political Behavior and the 2020 Elections," eJewish Philanthropy, October 12, 2020, https://ejewishphilanthropy.com/american-jewish-political-behavior-and-the-2020-elections/.

12 Ron Kampeas, "Meet the Top 15 Jewish Political Donors in This Election Cycle," Jewish Telegraphic Agency, September 14, 2020, https://www.jta.org/2020/09/24/politics/meet-the-top-15-jewish-political-donors.

Chapter 7

1   Doug Rossinow, "'The Edge of the Abyss': The Origins of the Israel Lobby, 1949–1954," *Modern American History* 1 (March 2018): 23–43, https://www.cambridge.org/core/services/aop-cambridge-core/content/view/E1690BDB5CA87C66B2B6512CA1D716A/S2515045617000177a.pdf/div-class-title-the-edge-of-the-abyss-the-origins-of-the-israel-lobby-1949-1954-div.pdf.

2   Ibid.

3   Amir Tibon, "Poll: American Support for Israel at Highest Rates Since Early 1990s as Partisan Gap Widens," *Haaretz*, May 14, 2018, https://www.haaretz.com/us-news/poll-results-americans-favor-israel-at-highest-rates-since-1990s-1.5905998.

4   Steven T. Rosenthal, *Irreconcilable Differences? The Waning of the American Jewish Love Affair with Israel* (Hanover, NH: Brandeis University Press, 2001), 93; and "The Second Intifada 2000," Anti-Defamation League, https://www.adl.org/resources/glossary-terms/the-second-intifada-2000.

5   Marilyn Cooper, ed., "The Growing Gap between Israel and American Jews," *Moment*, August 21, 2018, https://momentmag.com/growing-gap-israel-american-jews/.

6   "A Free Trip to Israel: Taglit," Birthright Israel, https://www.birthrightisrael.com/about-us.

7   Israel Nitzan, deputy consul general for the Israeli Consulate in New York, actively reaches out to rising leaders, including us.

8   AICF also does inspire American philanthropy to Israel.

9   Emily Burack, "7 Female Israeli Writers You Should Be Reading," Alma, March 5, 2017, https://www.heyalma.com/7-female-israeli-writers-you-should-be-reading/.

10 Pew Research Center, "American and Israeli Jews: Twin Portraits from Pew Research Center Surveys," Pew Research Center, January 24, 2017, https://www.pewforum.org/essay/american-and-israeli-jews-twin-portraits-from-pew-research-center-surveys/.

Chapter 8

1   Numbers 11:10–30, New Jewish Publication Society translation.

2   Numbers 11:29, adapted from the New Jewish Publication Society translation.

3　Joanna Ware, ed., "New Jewish Foundation Dedicates Millions to Jewish Social Justice Movement," Jewish Liberation Fund, November 30, 2020, https://www.jewishliberation.fund/news/jlf-launch-press-release.

4　Alana Semuels, "The Problem with Modern Philanthropy," *Atlantic*, March 28, 2017, https://www.theatlantic.com/business/archive/2017/03/the-problem-with-philanthropy/520989/.

5　"Rabbis Without Borders," Clal—The National Jewish Center for Learning and Leadership, https://www.clal.org/project/rabbis-without-borders/.

6　The quote is from the prior program description of the Hadrachah Seminar. This link has since been taken down: https://urj.org/what-we-do/hadrachah. Here is another reflection on the Hadrachah Seminar, for reference: Ken Hahn, "Had'Rachah: Inspiring Congregants to Lead," Union for Reform Judaism, April 29, 2015, https://urj.org/blog/hadrachah-inspiring-congregants-lead.

7　"OU Women's Initiative Holds First Lay Leadership Summit," Orthodox Union, May 23, 2019, https://www.ou.org/news/ou-womens-initiative-holds-first-lay-leadership-summit/.

8　Rising Song Institute, https://www.risingsong.org/.

9　"Become a Mikveh Guide," ImmerseNYC, http://www.immersenyc.org/becomeamikvehguide.

Chapter 9

1　For more, see Exodus 18.

2　This background information and quotes from Salazar in this chapter are from an interview conducted on December 13, 2020.

3　Armin Rosen, "Who Is Julia Salazar?," *Tablet*, August 23, 2018, https://www.tablet-mag.com/sections/news/articles/who-is-julia-salazar.

4　Karol Markowicz, "Opinion: Why Do Politicians Keep Lying about Their Heritage?," *Forward*, October 15, 2018, https://forward.com/opinion/412070/why-do-politicians-keep-lying-about-their-heritage/.

5　Tana Ganeva, "This Is the Story of How a Campaign Goes Off the Rails," *Rolling Stone*, September 11, 2018, https://www.rollingstone.com/politics/politics-features/julia-salazar-new-york-722616/; and Adam Jaffe et al., "We Are Julia Salazar's Former Classmates. We Had to Speak Out," *Forward*, September 5, 2018, https://forward.com/opinion/letters/409680/we-are-julia-salazars-former-classmates-we-had-to-speak-out/.

6　Dr. Clement Price regularly affirmed in dialogue with Rabbi Joshua Stanton that "race is a social construct." Even if so, the way in which society approaches race does not change on the basis of individual affiliation as much as longer-term societal trends. For this reason, we do not group race, sexual orientation, immigration status, etc. with characteristics that one can select oneself, such as political affiliation. For more on Professor Price's work, see "Clement Alexander Price, 1945–2014," Rutgers University, November 5, 2014, https://www.newark.rutgers.edu/news/clement-alexander-price-1945-2014.

7　David Schraub, "White Jews: An Intersectional Approach," *AJS Review* 43, no. 2 (2019): 379–407, https://www.cambridge.org/core/journals/ajs-review/article/white-jews-an-intersectional-approach/B3A8D66A0B6895A61814047FE406A2A6.

8　"Jews of Color: Who Counts, What We Ask, and Why It Matters," Jews of Color Field Building Initiative (Tides Center, May 2019), https://jewsofcolorfield building.org/wp-content/uploads/2019/05/JOC_bro_052119.pdf. While a recent

Pew study indicates a lower number, the scholarly consensus appears to be that the number of Jews of Color is rising significantly.

9   Asaf Shalev, "Without Using the Term, Pew Survey Unveils New Data on 'Jews of Color,'" *Jewish Telegraphic Agency*, May 11, 2021, https://www.jta.org/2021/05/11/ united-states/without-using-the-term-pew-survey-unveils-new-data-on-jews-of-color.

10   Pew Research Center, "Race, Ethnicity, Heritage, and Immigration among U.S. Jews," chapter 9 in *Jewish Americans in 2020* (Washington, DC: Pew Research Center, May 14, 2021), https://www.pewforum.org/2021/05/11/race-ethnicity-heritage-and-immigration-among-u-s-jews/; and Ari Feldman, "Jews of Color Have Been Consistently Undercounted by the American Jewish Establishment. Until Now," *Forward*, May 30, 2019, https://forward.com/news/national/425129/ jews-of-color-survey-jewish-population/.

11   This content is from an interview conducted with Zubeida Ullah-Eilenberg on January 18, 2021.

12   This content is from an interview conducted with Rabbi Mike Moskowitz on December 23, 2020.

13   The Babylonian Talmud frequently celebrates difference of perspective as the pathway to wisdom. *Bava M'tzia* 84a shows Rabbi Yochanan weeping over the death of his study partner because he would challenge his every idea. *B'rachot* 58a elevates diversity as something worthy of blessing: "Who sees crowds of Israelites should say, 'Blessed . . . who art wise in secrets,' because their minds differ and their faces differ."

14   Katherine W. Phillips, Kate A. Liljenquist, and Margaret A. Neale, "Is the Pain Worth the Gain? The Advantages and Liabilities of Agreeing with Socially Distinct Newcomers," *Personality and Social Psychology Bulletin* 35, no. 3 (2009): 336–50, https://journals.sagepub.com/doi/abs/10.1177/0146167208328062.

Chapter 10

1   Babylonian Talmud, *Makot* 24b; for the sake of clarity for the reader, we have paraphrased Rabbi Akiva's use of quotes from the biblical prophets Isaiah, Micah, and Zechariah. As prior prophets predicted the fall of the Temple, so too did they see such destruction as a precursor to a new rebuilding and renewal of Judaism.

2   Ten percent of American Jews say they were raised Orthodox, while only 8 percent identify as such today; 28 percent of American Jews say they were raised Reform, and 33 percent identify as such today. Jacob Ausubel, Gregory A. Smith, and Alan Cooperman, "Denominational Switching among U.S. Jews," Pew Research Center, June 22, 2021, https://www.pewresearch.org/fact-tank/ 2021/06/22/denominational-switching-among-u-s-jews-reform-judaism-has-gained-conservative-judaism-has-lost/.

3   Pew Research Center, "Marriage, Families and Children among U.S. Jews," chapter 4 in *Jewish Americans in 2020* (Washington, DC: Pew Research Center, May 20, 2021), https://www.pewforum.org/2021/05/11/marriage-families-and-children/.

4   Hadas Binyamini, "Philanthropy and the 'Jewish Continuity Crisis,'" Public Books, April 6, 2021, https://www.publicbooks.org/philanthropy-and-the-jewish-continuity-crisis/.

5   Alan Cooperman, ed., *A Portrait of Jewish Americans* (Washington, DC: Pew Research Center, October 1, 2013), https://www.pewforum.org/2013/10/01/ jewish-american-beliefs-attitudes-culture-survey/.

6   It should be noted that the 2020 study emphasizes methodological differences with the 2013 study. The study likewise might undercount Jews of Color, as it suggests that only 8 percent of people surveyed do not identify as white, in contrast to the Stanford University study that estimated twice that number.

7   Pew Research Center, *Jewish Americans in 2020* (Washington, DC: Pew Research Center, May 14, 2021), https://www.pewforum.org/2021/05/11/jewish-americans-in-2020/.

8   Ibid.

9   Pew Research Center, "The Size of the U.S. Jewish Population," chapter 1 in *Jewish Americans in 2020*, https://www.pewforum.org/2021/05/11/the-size-of-the-u-s-jewish-population/.

10   Drew Himmelstein, "1 in 6 American Jews Are Converts and 9 Other Findings in Pew Study," *J.: The Jewish News of Northern California*, March 15, 2015, https://www.jweekly.com/2015/05/15/1-in-6-american-jews-are-converts-and-9-other-findings-in-pew-study/. Informally, we have received corroboration for this possibility.

11   Pew Research Center, "Jewish Identity and Belief," chapter 2 in *Jewish Americans in 2020*, https://www.pewforum.org/2021/05/11/jewish-identity-and-belief/. We are grateful to Rabbis Julia Appel, Elan Babchuck, Brad Hirschfield, and Irwin Kula for their reflections on this Pew study and its significance.

12   Leviticus Rabbah 22:4.

13   Joseph Schumpeter, "Creative Destruction in Times of Covid," *Economist*, May 16, 2020, https://www.economist.com/business/2020/05/16/creative-destruction-in-times-of-covid.

Chapter 11

1   1 Samuel 1.

2   Babylonian Talmud, *B'rachot* 31a.

3   *Encyclopedia Britannica Online*, s.v. "Isaac Mayer Wise," https://www.britannica.com/biography/Isaac-Mayer-Wise; and Isaac Mayer Wise, *Minhag America: The Daily Prayers for American Israelites* (Cincinnati: Bloch, 1857), http://collections.americanjewisharchives.org/wise/attachment/5329/theDailyPrayersFinal.pdf.

4   *Seder Tefilot Yiśra'el: The Union Prayer Book for Jewish Worship, Part II* (Cincinnati: Central Conference of American Rabbis, 1894), https://babel.hathitrust.org/cgi/pt?id=hvd.hwmctm&view=1up&seq=5&skin=2021.

5   Barnett A. Elzas, *The Organ in the Synagogue: An Interesting Chapter in the History of Reform Judaism in America* (early 1900s [precise date unknown]), available through the Open Collections Program at Harvard University, https://curiosity.lib.harvard.edu/immigration-to-the-united-states-1789-1930/catalog/39-990000695180203941.

6   Michael Feldberg, "The First Bat Mitzvah in the United States (March 18, 1922)," Jewish Virtual Library, https://www.jewishvirtuallibrary.org/the-first-bat-mitzvah-in-the-united-states.

7   Vanessa Ochs, *Inventing Jewish Ritual* (Philadelphia: Jewish Publication Society, 2007), 42.

8   Mark Oppenheimer, "DIY Judaism," *Tablet*, February 27, 2017, https://www.tabletmag.com/sections/news/articles/diy-judaism.

9   Ibid.

10   "The Reconstructionist movement had appropriated this term in the early 1960s in an effort to promote the creation of small fellowship circles consisting of Jews who were partial to the ideas of Mordecai Kaplan [the founder of Reconstructionist Judaism] and gathered on a regular basis for study, discussion, and prayer." These were countercultural Jewish communities, which spurned bourgeoisie notions of suburban synagogue life from the postwar era. For more, see Jonathan Sarna, *American Judaism: A History* (New Haven, CT: Yale University Press, 2005).

11   Vanessa Ochs, *Inventing Jewish Ritual* (New York: Jewish Publication Society, 2014), 43.

12   Sarna, *American Judaism*, 321.

13   Ibid.

14   "Our Story," Moishe House, February 15, 2021, https://www.moishehouse.org/about-us/our-story/.

15   This content is from an interview conducted with Mr. Cygielman on January 6, 2021.

16   Lori Hope Lefkovitz and Rona Shapiro, "Ritualwell.Org—Loading the Virtual Canon, or: The Politics and Aesthetics of Jewish Women's Spirituality," *Nashim: A Journal of Jewish Women's Studies & Gender Issues* 9 (2005): 101–25, http://doi.org/10.1353/nsh.2005.0005.

17   Ibid.

18   Ibid.

19   Ochs, *Inventing Jewish Ritual*, 47–55.

20   Jeri Zeder, "How Summer Camp Became a Jewish Thing," My Jewish Learning, https://www.myjewishlearning.com/article/summer-camps/.

21   Michael M. Lorge and Gary P. Zola, eds., *A Place of Our Own: The Rise of Reform Jewish Camping* (Tuscaloosa: University of Alabama Press, 2006), 17.

22   Ibid., 17–18.

23   Donald Splansky, "Creating a Prayer Experience in Reform Jewish Camps and Beyond," in Lorge and Zola, *A Place of Our Own*, 153.

24   Judah M. Cohen, "Singing Out for Judaism," in Lorge and Zola, *A Place of Our Own*, 177.

25   Ibid., 187–96.

26   Ibid.

27   Judah M. Cohen, "'And the Youth Shall See Visions . . .': Summer Camps, Song-leading, and Musical Identity among American Reform Jewish Teenagers," in *Musical Childhoods and Cultures of Youth*, ed. Susan Boynton and Roe-Min Kok (Middletown, CT: Wesleyan University Press, 2006), 188–91.

28   Ibid., 200.

29   It should be noted that Rabbi Carlebach also had a "shadow side" of misconduct. For more, see Sarah Blaustein, "Rabbi Shlomo Carlebach's Shadow Side," *Lilith*, March 9, 1998, https://lilith.org/articles/rabbi-shlomo-carlebachs-shadow-side/.

30   Margalit Fox, "Debbie Friedman, Singer of Jewish Music, Dies at 59," *New York Times*, January 11, 2011, https://www.nytimes.com/2011/01/11/arts/music/11friedman.html.

31   Rosalie Will, "Register Now for Hava Nashira 2021," Union for Reform Judaism, May 13, 2021, https://urj.org/blog/register-now-hava-nashira-2021.

32   "Here's Everything You Can Expect from Hava Nashira 2020," Union for Reform Judaism, February 10, 2020, https://urj.org/blog/heres-everything-you-can-expect-hava-nashira-2020.

33 Ibid.

34 "Learn with Hadar," Hadar Institute, https://www.hadar.org/yeshivat-hadar.

35 "Rising Song Institute," Hadar Institute, https://www.risingsong.org/.

36 "Rising Song Circles," Joey Weisenberg, https://joey-weisenberg.mykajabi.com/rising-song-circles.

37 Jesse Bernstein, "NMAJH Uses Music to Bridge Pandemic Gaps," *Jewish Exponent*, July 1, 2020, https://www.jewishexponent.com/2020/07/01/nmajh-uses-music-to-bridge-pandemic-gaps/.

38 Renee Ghert-Zand, "With Eye on Jewish Continuity, Maverick Spiritual Leader Goes Mainstream," Times of Israel, May 17, 2016, https://www.timesofisrael.com/with-eye-on-jewish-continuity-maverick-spiritual-leader-goes-mainstream/.

39 "Translator" and subsequent quotes are from an interview conducted with Rabbi Amichai Lau-Lavie on February 3, 2021.

40 "Storahtelling," Lab/Shul, https://labshul.org/storahtelling/.

41 BimBam was formerly known as G-dcast.

42 "Leadership Profile: Sarah Lefton," Bernstein Family Foundation, https://bernsteinfamilyfoundationdc.org/sarah-lefton/.

43 Ibid.

44 "Judaism 101," BimBam, https://www.bimbam.com/judaism-101/.

45 Sarah Lefton, "What's Innovative and Explosively Creative? Standards," eJewish Philanthropy, March 5, 2019, https://ejewishphilanthropy.com/whats-innovative-and-explosively-creative-standards/.

46 "Reformjudaism.org Becomes New Home for Bimbam Content," eJewish Philanthropy, April 2, 2019, https://ejewishphilanthropy.com/reformjudaism-org-becomes-new-home-for-bimbam-content/.

47 "BimBam Bids Farewell," BimBam, https://www.bimbam.com/bimbam-bids-farewell/.

48 The other four leaders of the quintet have also contributed to Jewish leadership in multiple realms: Nancy Flam, Susan Friedman, Ellen Hermanson, and Nessa Rapoport.

49 "Rachel Cowan," Jewish Women's Archive, https://jwa.org/feminism/cowan-rachel.

50 Ibid.

51 "Our Staff, Teachers, and Board," Institute for Jewish Spirituality, https://www.jewishspirituality.org/about/our-staff-teachers-and-board/. At the time of IJS's founding, Rabbi Cowan was serving as a beloved staff member of the Nathan Cummings Foundation: https://nathancummings.org/remembering-rabbi-rachel-cowan/.

52 "About the Institute for Jewish Spirituality," Institute for Jewish Spirituality, https://www.jewishspirituality.org/about/.

53 "Remembering Rabbi Rachel Cowan," Nathan Comings Foundation, February 11, 2019, https://nathancummings.org/remembering-rabbi-rachel-cowan/.

54 Rabbi Dr. Joshua Feigelson, IJS's current executive director, has broken new ground and brought countless resources and learning opportunities online.

55 In the closing chapters of her life, Rabbi Cowan coauthored with Dr. Linda Thal *Wise Aging: Living with Joy, Resilience, and Spirit* (Springfield, NJ: Behrman House, 2015) to inspire aging adults to find greater meaning and live with renewed purpose. It was a fitting Festschrift to her tireless work to unearth Jewish practices to help elevate life's many moments and stages.

56 Sam Kestenbaum, "In the Jewish Self-Help Known as 'Mussar' Students Find Election-Year Succor," *Forward*, November 13, 2016, https://forward.com/news/353410/can-19th-century-jewish-self-help-credo-of-mussar-help-you-cope-with-donald/.

57 Rahel Musleah, "Mussar: Jewish Spirituality for the Modern World," *Hadassah Magazine*, March 8, 2017, https://www.hadassahmagazine.org/2017/01/12/mussar-jewish-spirituality-modern-world/.

Chapter 12

1 Genesis 11:6, New Jewish Publication Society translation.

2 Babylonian Talmud, *Megillah* 29a, Sefaria, https://www.sefaria.org/Deuteronomy.30.3?lang=bi&with=Megillah&lang2=en.

3 Beth Wenger, "Mikveh," Jewish Women's Archive, June 23, 2021, https://jwa.org/encyclopedia/article/mikveh.

4 Heteronormativity remains within a large segment of Orthodox Judaism.

5 Allison Hoffman, "The New American Mikveh," *Tablet*, https://www.tabletmag.com/sections/belief/articles/the-new-american-mikveh.

6 Sue Fishkoff, "Reimagining the Mikveh," *Reform Judaism Magazine*, Fall 2008, https://reformjudaism.org/reimagining-mikveh.

7 Hoffman, "The New American Mikveh."

8 Elicia Brown, "NYC Takes the Plunge," *Jewish Week*, October 13, 2014, https://jewishweek.timesofisrael.com/nyc-takes-the-plunge/.

9 Avital Chizhik-Goldschmidt, "The Mikveh Is the Trendy Place to Be, in Manhattan's Upper West Side," *Forward*, August 28, 2018, https://forward.com/life/409055/the-mikveh-is-the-trendy-place-to-be-in-manhattans-upper-west-side/.

10 Izzy Abrahmson, "Local Nonprofit Is Making Matzah on a Mission," *Providence Monthly*, March 25, 2021, https://providenceonline.com/stories/local-nonprofit-is-making-matzah-on-a-mission,36789.

11 "Mitzvah Matzos: Matzos on a Mission," Mitzvah Matzos, https://www.mitzvahmatzos.org/.

12 This is from our interview with Rabbi Barry Dolinger on February 19, 2021.

13 Mark Gerson, *The Telling: How Judaism's Essential Book Reveals the Meaning of Life* (New York: St. Martin's Essentials, 2021), 13. Mark is also an entrepreneur, chairman of United Hatzalah, and a member of Congregation Rodeph Sholom in New York City.

14 During the Covid-19 pandemic, Haggadot.com expanded its offerings to include a HighHolidays@Home website, with opportunities for learning, connection, and co-creation of ritual. For more, see Courtney Rubin, "Celebrate the Jewish High Holy Days, Pandemic-Style," *New York Times*, September 6, 2020, https://www.nytimes.com/2020/09/06/at-home/celebrate-jewish-holidays-safely-coronavirus.html.

15 This is an approximation of the authors, based on public data on usership of Haggadot.com. If there are one hundred thousand users creating materials, those materials are distributed to countless additional family, friends, community members, etc.

16 "Mission and Vision," Haggadot.com, https://www.haggadot.com/about/mission.

17   Judy Bolton-Fasman, "Customizing a Haggadah Is Free and Accessible,"
      JewishBoston, March 16, 2021, https://www.jewishboston.com/read/customizing-
      a-haggadah-is-free-and-accessible/.

18   Ibid.

19   The other cofounder is Rabbi Joshua Stanton, who at the time was an undergraduate.

Chapter 13

1   Rabbi Joshua Stanton was her sponsoring rabbi for conversion and separately
      interviewed her for this book.

2   "Conservative Rabbis Rule on Streaming Services on Shabbat and Yom Tov,"
      Rabbinical Assembly, May 14, 2020, https://www.rabbinicalassembly.org/story/
      conservative-rabbis-rule-streaming-services-shabbat-and-yom-tov.

3   These data are publicly available on Central Synagogue's YouTube channel and
      Facebook page.

4   Josefin Dolsten, "For now, online services mean many synagogues are seeing
      greater attendance," Times of Israel, April 24, 2020, https://www.timesofisrael.
      com/for-now-online-services-mean-many-synagogues-are-seeing-greater-
      attendance/.

5   This holds true of our synagogues, as of this draft on October 29, 2021.

6   In contrast to "nostalgia," we suggest that this phenomenon relates to knowing
      where one comes from and the ongoing search for "authenticity," rather than a
      glorified vision of the past.

7   For more on one notion of a "community without walls," see Dan Aubrey, "How a
      Community without Walls Was Built," Princeton Info, November 25, 2020, https://
      princetoninfo.com/how-a-community-without-walls-was-built/.

8   Mark Oppenheimer, "Surprising Trends Driving Conversion to Judaism,"
      Tablet, May 13, 2021, https://www.tabletmag.com/sections/community/articles/
      conversion-not-just-for-marriage-anymore.

Chapter 14

1   "Al Vorspan, z"l," Religious Action Center of Reform Judaism, February 2019,
      https://rac.org/al-vorspan-zl.

2   "Rabbi Maurice N. Eisendrath," Union for American Hebrew Congregations (now
      the Union for Reform Judaism), 1973, https://urj.org/what-we-believe/resolutions/
      rabbi-maurice-n-eisendrath.

3   Steven Cohen and Leonard Fein, American Jews and Their Social Justice Involvement:
      Evidence from a National Survey (Amos—The National Jewish Partnership
      for Social Justice, November 21, 2001), https://www.bjpa.org/search-results/
      publication/4692; much of this is reinforced by Pew Research Center, "Jewish
      Identity and Belief," chapter 2 in Jewish Americans in 2020 (Washington, DC:
      Pew Research Center, 2021), https://www.pewforum.org/2021/05/11/jewish-
      identity-and-belief/.

4   It is important to note that many right-wing Jews similarly feel disenfranchised
      by mainstream Jewish organizations. Places like the Republican Jewish Coalition
      have become gathering places for the 20–25 percent of American Jews who identi-
      fy as Republican and often feel as though they do not have a place in the main-
      stream of Jewish life, which tends to be more centrist or center-left. For more,
      see David Schechter, "Jewish Voters Bring Historic Trends and Concerns," Atlanta

Jewish Times, October 16, 2020, https://atlantajewishtimes.timesofisrael.com/jewish-voters-bring-historic-trends-and-concerns/. There are many similar articles on the subject in other publications, as well.

5   The interview with Audrey Sasson took place on February 10, 2021.

6   The interview with Morriah Kaplan took place on January 15, 2021.

7   This is the figure that Morriah Kaplan quoted, as of January 15, 2021.

8   Pew Research Center, *Jewish Americans in 2020* (Washington, DC: Pew Research Center, May 11, 2021), https://www.pewforum.org/2021/05/11/jewish-americans-in-2020/.

9   Josh Nathan-Kazis, "'Zioness' Group Adds Pro-Israel Voice to Racial Justice Marches—and Sows Bitter Controversy," *Forward*, October 5, 2017, https://forward.com/news/384385/zioness-group-adds-pro-israel-voice-to-racial-justice-marches-and-sows/.

10 The interview with Amanda Berman took place on February 10, 2021.

11 As noted by Amanda Berman, no other symbols were barred from the march that year.

12 Aiden Pink, "DC Dyke March Bans Jewish Pride Flag," *Forward*, June 6, 2019, https://forward.com/fast-forward/425533/dc-dyke-march-bans-jewish-pride-flag/.

Chapter 15

1   The interview with Rabbi Leon Morris took place on January 18, 2021.

2   "About," Hadar Institute, https://www.hadar.org/about.

3   The interview with Rabbi Kaunfer took place on January 6, 2021.

4   The interview with Rabbi Kaunfer took place on January 6, 2021.

5   "About," Hadar Institute.

6   Ibid.

7   The interview with Rabbi Kaunfer took place on January 6, 2021.

8   The interview with David Singer took place on January 7, 2021.

9   "About," Limmud North America, https://limmudna.org/about/.

10 "What We Do," Limmud North America, https://limmudna.org/programs/.

11 "About," Limmud North America.

12 Sharon Weiss-Greenberg provided this data via email on May 6, 2021.

13 Ibid.

14 Simon Rocker, "The Greatest Jewish Website in the World," *Jewish Chronicle*, December 23, 2019, https://www.thejc.com/news/uk/the-greatest-jewish-website-in-the-world-1.494665.

15 "Featured Grants: Sefaria," William Davidson Foundation, https://williamdavidson.org/featured-grants/sefaria/#:~:text=Sefaria's%20founders%2C%20the%20best%2Dselling,to%20the%20entire%20Jewish%20canon.

16 Shira Hanau, "After Digitizing the Talmud, Sefaria Seeks to Do the Same to Democracy," *J.: The Jewish News of Northern California*, July 14, 2020, https://www.jweekly.com/2020/07/14/after-digitizing-the-talmud-sefaria-seeks-to-do-the-same-to-democracy/.

17 For more, see "Featured Grants: Sefaria," William Davidson Foundation, https://williamdavidson.org/featured-grants/sefaria/#:~:text=Sefaria's%20founders%2C%20the%20best%2Dselling,to%20the%20entire%20Jewish%20canon.

18 Noah Smith, "The Quest to Put the Talmud Online," *Washington Post*, September 18, 2018, https://www.washingtonpost.com/religion/2018/09/18/quest-put-talmud-online/.

19 "About," Sefaria, https://www.sefaria.org/about.

20 Smith, "Quest to Put the Talmud Online."

21 "About," Sefaria.

22 Dr. Judith Plaskow's landmark 1990 book *Standing Again at Sinai* (San Francisco: HarperCollins) continues to transform feminist Torah study. The Jewish Women's Archive features Rabbi Rachel Adler's insightful reflections on Dr. Plaskow's life and professional contributions (last updated June 23, 2021): https://jwa.org/encyclopedia/article/plaskow-judith.

23 Women of Reform Judaism commissioned *The Torah: A Women's Commentary*, edited by Dr. Tamara Cohen Eskenazi and Andrea L. Weiss. Here is a brief reflection from Women of Reform Judaism on the process and early outcomes of the landmark commentary: https://wrj.org/torah-womens-commentary-0.

24 This is Hurwitz's chosen designation as clergy, a feminine conjugation of the term "Rabbi."

25 "Mission," Yeshivat Maharat, https://www.yeshivatmaharat.org/mission-and-p2.

26 Ibid.

27 The interview with Rabba Hurwitz took place on January 13, 2021.

28 The interview with Dr. Rosenbaum took place on February 8, 2021.

Chapter 16

1 This has held especially true during the Covid-19 pandemic. OneTable issued the report *Alone, Less Lonely* in February 2021 to see if even virtual Shabbat experiences could bring a sense of connection and reduce isolation: https://issuu.com/onetableshabbat/docs/alone__less_lonely__1_.

2 *Beyond Scale: A Report on Impact,* OneTable, https://onetable.org/Reports/Beyond_Scale.pdf.

3 Ibid.

4 Graham Wright, Shahar Hecht, and Leonard Saxe, *Jewish Futures Project: Birthright Israel's First Decade of Applicants; A Look at the Long-Term Program Impact* (Waltham, MA: Cohen Center for Modern Jewish Studies at Brandeis University, November 2020), https://bir.brandeis.edu/bitstream/handle/10192/39072/jewish-futures-wave6-110620.pdf.

5 Ibid.

6 Ibid., 12.

7 Alan Cooperman, ed., *A Portrait of Jewish Americans* (Washington, DC: Pew Research Center October 1, 2013), https://www.pewforum.org/2013/10/01/jewish-american-beliefs-attitudes-culture-survey/.

8 "About Us," Honeymoon Israel, https://honeymoonisrael.org/about-us/.

9 Joe Kanfer, "The Heart and Science of Building Community through Honeymoon Israel," Slingshot Fund, September 8, 2020, https://www.slingshotfund.org/post/the-heart-and-science-of-building-community-through-honeymoon-israel/.

10 "Around the World," PJ Library, https://pjlibrary.org/about-pj-library/pj-around-the-world.

11 "Intermarriage and Other Demographics," chapter 2 in Cooperman, *A Portrait of Jewish Americans*, https://www.pewforum.org/2013/10/01/chapter-2-intermarriage-and-other-demographics/.

12 This data is based on our interview with Jodi Bromberg, CEO of 18Doors, on February 4, 2021.

13 18Doors is its current name, but the same organization has remained in continual operation since 1998.

Chapter 17

1 Douglas Martin, "Clement A. Price, a Cheerleader for Newark, Dies at 69," *New York Times*, November 8, 2014, https://www.nytimes.com/2014/11/09/nyregion/clement-a-price-a-cheerleader-for-newark-dies-at-69.html.

2 Erin Cooley et al., "The Fluid Perception of Racial Identity: The Role of Friendship Groups," *Social Psychological and Personality Science* 9, no. 1 (2018): 32–39, https://doi.org/10.1177/1948550617703171.

3 For more on this particular permutation of identities, we recommend Rodger Kamenetz's bestselling book *The Jew in the Lotus* (New York: HarperCollins, 1994).

4 This describes one of our recent conversion students, who is deeply, soulfully Jewish and fully Chinese as well.

5 Susan Katz Miller, *Being Both: Embracing Two Religions in One Interfaith Family* (Boston: Beacon Press, 2013), 17.

6 Rabbi Brad Hirschfield was among the first people we have heard who used the term "Jewish" and "wisdom tradition" in the same sentence.

7 For example, see Northeastern Hillel's "About Us" page: https://www.northeasternhillel.org/about-us.html.

8 "About," Clal—The National Jewish Center for Learning and Leadership, https://www.clal.org/pages/about/.

9 Rabbi David Gelfand first introduced us to the notion of formal conversion as gaining "citizenship" within the Jewish people.

10 Vanessa Ochs, introduction to *The Book of Jewish Sacred Practices: CLAL's Guide to Everyday & Holiday Rituals and Blessings*, ed. Irwin Kula and Vanessa Ochs (Woodstock, VT: Jewish Lights, 2001), 5.

11 Isaiah 42:6, New Jewish Publication Society translation.

Chapter 18

1 Robert Wuthnow, *After Heaven: Spirituality in America Since the 1950s* (Berkeley: University of California Press, 1998), 4.

2 Mel Scult, *The Radical American Judaism of Mordecai M. Kaplan* (Bloomington: University of Indiana Press, 2015), 10.

3 "History," Jewish Center, http://www.jewishcenter.org/history.html. The Jewish Center is not to be confused with the Society for the Advancement of Judaism, which Kaplan founded in 1922 as an exploration of new approaches in bringing Judaism into modern American life through synagogue community.

4   *American Jewish Year Book* 64 (1963): 145. Some studies, like that of Marshall Sklare and Joseph Greenbaum's *Jewish Identity on the Suburban Frontier: A Study of Group Survival in the Open Society,* 2nd rev. ed. (Chicago: University of Chicago Press, 1979), suggest that number may have been even higher.

5   Pew Research Center, "Jewish Practices and Customs," chapter 3 in *Jewish Americans in 2020* (Washington, DC: Pew Research Center, 2021), https://www.pewforum.org/2021/05/11/jewish-practices-and-customs/.

6   Alan Cooperman, ed., *A Portrait of Jewish Americans* (Washington, DC: Pew Research Center, October 1, 2013), 52, https://www.pewresearch.org/wp-content/uploads/sites/7/2013/10/jewish-american-full-report-for-web.pdf. We thank our teachers from Clal—The National Jewish Center for Learning and Leadership for emphasizing this data point during Rabbis Without Borders retreats.

7   "Jewish Identity," chapter 3 in Cooperman, *A Portrait of Jewish Americans,* http://www.pewforum.org/2013/10/01/chapter-3-jewish-identity/.

8   Josh Packard et al., *Belonging: Reconnecting America's Loneliest Generation* (Bloomington, MN: Springtide Research Institute, 2020).

9   D'Vera Cohn et al., "Barely Half of U.S. Adults Are Married—A Record Low," Pew Research Center's Social & Demographic Trends Project (Pew Research Center, August 27, 2020), https://www.pewresearch.org/social-trends/2011/12/14/barely-half-of-u-s-adults-are-married-a-record-low/.

10   Sid Schwartz, *Jewish Megatrends: Charting the Course of the American Jewish Future* (Woodstock, VT: Jewish Lights, 2013), 3.

11   "Rabbi Paul Yedwab," Temple Israel (West Bloomfield, MI), https://www.temple-israel.org/clergy/rabbi-paul-yedwab.

12   Paul Yedwab, "Inserting a 'Disruptor' into the Jewish Spiritual Marketplace," *CCAR Journal: The Reform Jewish Quarterly,* Winter 2017, https://www.ccarnet.org/winter-2017/.

13   The interview with Rabbi Paul Yedwab took place on January 4, 2021.

14   One such venture, known as "The Well" was named one of the top fifty most innovative Jewish organizations in 2018. For more, see Jackie Headapohl, "A Pioneering Organization," *Detroit Jewish News,* June 14, 2018, https://thejewishnews.com/2018/06/14/a-pioneering-organization-the-well/.

15   Eleyna Fugma, "A Place at the Table—A Report from TischPDX: Unaffiliated Jewish Leadership Incubator," eJewish Philanthropy, March 19, 2021, https://ejewishphilanthropy.com/a-place-at-the-table-a-report-from-tischpdx-unaffiliated-jewish-leadership-incubator/.

16   "Uplifting Bold Leaders: Eleyna Fugman: TischPDX," Upstart, November 12, 2020, https://upstartlab.org/uplifting-bold-leaders-eleyna-fugman/?utm_source=TischPDX&utm_campaign=23b770de84-EMAIL_CAMPAIGN_2020_12_10_09_51&utm_medium=email&utm_term=0_cf60dc730e-23b770de84-47629107.

Chapter 19

1   Leonard Saxe et al., *American Jewish Population Estimates 2020* (Waltham, MA: Steinhardt Social Research Institute at Brandeis University, 2021), 11, https://ajpp.brandeis.edu/us_jewish_population_2020.

2   "Network Communities," Jewish Federations of North America, https://jewishfederations.org/network-communities.

3   Rachel Isaacs, "Small Town Jewish Life Takes Center Stage," eJewish Philanthropy, June 11, 2019, https://ejewishphilanthropy.com/small-town-jewish-life-takes-center-stage/.

4   Ibid.

5   "Maine Conference for Jewish Life," Center for Small Town Jewish Life, https://jewishlife.colby.edu/maine-conference-for-jewish-life/.

6   Yonat Shimron, "Mississippi Institute Is an Anchor for Jewish Communities in the South," Faith and Leadership (Duke University Divinity School), July 12, 2016, https://faithandleadership.com/mississippi-institute-anchor-jewish-communities-south.

7   "Virtual Road Trip through the Jewish South," Institute for Southern Jewish Life, https://www.isjl.org/virtual-road-trip.html.

Chapter 20

1   Andrew Solomon, *Far from the Tree: Parents, Children and the Search for Identity* (New York: Scribner, 2012), 2, 47.

2   We brought forward this frame in our guest editors' introduction to *CCAR Journal: The Reform Jewish Quarterly*, Winter 2017, published by the Central Conference of American Rabbis.

3   Ron Csillag, "The Secrets of Chabad's Global Expansion," *Canadian Jewish News*, May 23, 2018, https://www.cjnews.com/living-jewish/the-secrets-of-chabads-global-expansion.

4   Steven Windmueller, "Unpacking Chabad: Their Ten Core Elements for Success," eJewish Philanthropy, August 2, 2012, http://ejpprod.wpengine.com/unpacking-chabad-their-ten-core-elements-for-success/.

5   Deborah Fineblum, "Millennials Search for Meaning and Authenticity When It Comes to Judaism," JNS, January 14, 2020, https://www.jns.org/millennials-search-for-meaning-and-authenticity-when-it-comes-to-judaism/.

6   "Our Story," Moishe House, https://www.moishehouse.org/about-us/our-story/.

7   Erin Ben-Moche, "Moishe House Absorbs Base Movement Network from Hillel International," *Jewish Journal*, March 5, 2021, https://jewishjournal.com/community/333892/moishe-house-absorbs-base-movement-network-from-hillel-international/.

8   Amy Sara Clark, "Reform-Led Chabad-Style House Opens in Brooklyn," *Jewish Week*, February 14, 2018, https://jewishweek.timesofisrael.com/the-new-sacred-circles/.

9   "A Conversation with Rabbi Sara Luria," Glean Network, January 18, 2018, https://www.gleannetwork.org/post/a-conversation-with-rabbi-sara-luria.

10   Elie Kaunfer, *Empowered Judaism: What Independent Minyanim Can Teach Us about Building Vibrant Jewish Communities* (Woodstock, VT: Jewish Lights, 2010).

11   JTA, "Young Jews Find Spirituality Outside the Synagogue," *Jerusalem Post*, August 13, 2017, https://www.jpost.com/diaspora/how-young-jews-find-spirituality-outside-the-synagogue-502290.

12   Kaunfer, *Empowered Judaism*, 61.

13   Ibid., 84.

14   "Shabbat in a Box," Livnot U'Lehibanot, https://www.livnot.org/wp-content/uploads/2017/05/Shabbat-in-a-box-A-Guide-for-Making-Shabbat.pdf.

15   Gabe Stutman, "Subscribers to Hello Mazel, Popular Jewish Kickstarter Project, Appear to Be Out of Luck," *J.: The Jewish News of Northern California,* June 21, 2019, https://www.jweekly.com/2019/06/21/subscribers-to-hello-mazel-most-popular-jewish-kickstarter-of-all-time-appear-to-be-out-of-luck/; and "Hipster Care Package Startup Sets Jewish Kickstarter Record at over $70K," Jewish Telegraphic Agency, February 14, 2016, https://www.jta.org/2016/02/14/united-states/hipster-care-package-startup-sets-kickstarter-record-for-jewish-campaign.

16   "Hipster Care Package Startup."

17   It should be noted that we are working on one of several start-ups in this space, creating something akin to a "Peloton of Jewish Ideas," along with Rabbi Elan Babchuck, director of innovation at Clal.

Chapter 21

1   Irving Greenberg, *The Third Great Cycle of Jewish History,* Perspectives (New York: Clal—The National Jewish Center for Learning and Leadership, 1981), 21.

2   Ibid.

3   "David Horovitz," Times of Israel, https://www.timesofisrael.com/writers/david-horovitz/.

4   The interview with David Horovitz took place on January 6, 2021.

5   We are experimenting with some in our respective communities, in collaboration with the Pardes Institute.

6   For more, see Jack Bloom, *The Rabbi as Symbolic Exemplar* (New York: Routledge, 2002).

Conclusion

1   Michael Lipka, "Attending a Seder Is Common Practice for American Jews," Pew Research Center, April 14, 2014, https://www.pewresearch.org/fact-tank/2014/04/14/attending-a-seder-is-common-practice-for-american-jews/.

2   Exodus 19:4, New Jewish Publication Society translation.

3   Kwon Ping Ho and Arnoud De Meyer, *The Art of Leadership* (Singapore: World Scientific, 2017), 170.

4   Rosabeth Moss Kanter, "Change Is Hardest in the Middle," *Harvard Business Review,* August 12, 2009, https://hbr.org/2009/08/change-is-hardest-in-the-middl.

5   Neel Burton, "Our Hierarchy of Needs," *Psychology Today,* May 23, 2012, https://www.psychologytoday.com/us/blog/hide-and-seek/201205/our-hierarchy-needs.

6   Richard Bulliet, *Islam: The View from the Edge* (New York: Columbia University Press, 1994), 169–77.

7   Literally, *d'rash* it.

8 . We are grateful to Professor Michael Marmur of the Hebrew Union College–Jewish Institute of Religion for teaching this text, which resides in the Mishnah, but not in the Talmud.

9   Jack Wertheimer, *The New Jewish Leaders: Reshaping the American Jewish Landscape* (Waltham, MA: Brandeis University Press, 2010), 324.

10   A census is not simply an instrument for self-understanding. In counting some people in, a census also counts others out. History is riddled with examples of

censuses that dehumanize. In Judaism, counting one's own people is every bit as fraught as counting another. Hosea 2:1 (New Jewish Publication Society translation) affirms, "The number of the people of Israel shall be like that of the sands of the sea, which cannot be measured or counted; and instead of being told, 'You are Not-My-People,' they shall be called 'Children-of-the-Living-God.'" Our sages then distinguish between measuring and counting, indicating that determinations of quality as well as number of people must not be conducted (Babylonian Talmud, *Yoma* 22b). Noting the inconsistency between these rules and the Book of Numbers, which is filled with multiple censuses of different groups, the medieval commentator Nachmanides deduces that any census must have a purpose and cannot simply be done for its own sake (see his commentary on Numbers 1:3). A census is an exercise of power and must be tempered by the higher purpose that it serves.

Appendix 1

1   Angie Thurston and Casper ter Kuile, *How We Gather*, April 2015, https://caspertk.files.wordpress.com/2015/04/how-we-gather.pdf.

2   Yonat Shimron, "Study: Jews of Color Love Judaism but Often Experience Racism in Jewish Settings," Religion News Service, August 12, 2021, https://religionnews.com/2021/08/12/study-jews-of-color-love-judaism-but-often-experience-racism-in-jewish-settings/.

3   "UJA-Federation of New York's Second Report on Synagogues Adopting Voluntary Dues Finds Trend Now Growing among Diverse Group of Congregations," UJA-Federation of New York, May 16, 2017, https://www.ujafedny.org/news/uja-federation-of-new-yorks-second-report-on-synagogues-adopting-voluntary-dues-finds-trend-now-growing-among-diverse-group-of-congregations.

4   Isaiah 56:7.

Appendix 2

1   As it is called in many Eurocentric texts.

2   "Timeline," American Jewish Archives, March 4, 2021, http://americanjewisharchives.org/education/timeline.php.

3   Ibid.

4   Avital Chizhik-Goldschmidt, "The Mikveh Is the Trendy Place to Be, in Manhattan's Upper West Side," *Forward*, August 28, 2018, https://forward.com/life/409055/the-mikveh-is-the-trendy-place-to-be-in-manhattans-upper-west-side/.

5   "Timeline," American Jewish Archives.

6   Julian E. Zelizer, "Trump Needs to Demilitarize His Rhetoric," *Atlantic*, October 29, 2018, https://www.theatlantic.com/ideas/archive/2018/10/americas-long-history-antisemitism/574234/.

7   Irving Greenberg, *The Third Great Cycle of Jewish History*, Perspectives (New York: Clal—The National Jewish Center for Learning and Leadership, 1981), https://rabbiirvinggreenberg.com/wp-content/uploads/2013/02/1Perspectives-3rd-Great-Cycle-1987-CLAL-1-of-3.pdf.

8   Jonathan Sarna, *American Judaism: A History* (New Haven, CT: Yale University Press, 2004), 75.

9   Alan M. Dershowitz, *The Vanishing American Jew* (New York: Simon and Schuster, 1998), 11.

10   Ibid., 277.

11   Pew Research Center, "Feelings toward Religious Groups," chapter 4 in *What Americans Know about Religion* (Washington, DC: Pew Research Center, July 23, 2019), https://www.pewforum.org/2019/07/23/feelings-toward-religious-groups/.

12   This is not to minimize antisemitism, but to push for us to hold the dual realities of antisemitism and philo-Semitism in the United States. "Antisemitism in the US," Anti-Defamation League, https://www.adl.org/what-we-do/antisemitism/antisemitism-in-the-us.

13   Michael Lipka, "A Closer Look at Jewish Identity in Israel and the U.S.," Pew Research Center, May 31, 2020, https://www.pewresearch.org/fact-tank/2016/03/16/a-closer-look-at-jewish-identity-in-israel-and-the-u-s/.

14   We might even venture to suggest that other religious communities in America experienced it as well.

15   Parts of this section on the Second Great Awakening stem from our op-ed in the Religion News Service: Benjamin Spratt and Joshua Stanton, "How a Supreme Court Bent on Protecting Religion Could Harm It," Religion News Service, December 1, 2020, https://religionnews.com/2020/12/01/how-a-supreme-court-bent-on-protecting-religion-could-harm-it/.

16   This included the Episcopalian and Presbyterian churches.

17   Steven Waldman, *Sacred Liberty: America's Long, Bloody, and Ongoing Struggle for Religious Freedom* (New York: HarperOne, 2019), 89.

18   The first two paragraphs of the section on the Great Awakening were adapted from the article that we coauthored for Religion News Service: Spratt and Stanton, "How a Supreme Court Bent on Protecting Religion Could Harm It."

19   Barry Hankins, *The Second Great Awakening and the Transcendentalists*, Greenwood Guides to Historic Events 1500–1900 (Westport, CT: Greenwood Press, 2004), 5.

20   Ibid.

21   William McLoughlin, *Revivals, Awakenings, and Reform: An Essay on Religion and Social Change in America, 1607–1977*, Chicago History of American Religion, ed. Martin Marty (Chicago: University of Chicago Press, 1978), 2.

22   Megan Brenan, "Religiosity Largely Unaffected by Events of 2020 in U.S.," Gallup, April 1, 2021, https://news.gallup.com/poll/341957/religiosity-largely-unaffected-events-2020.aspx?utm_source=alert&utm_medium=email&utm_content=morelink&utm_campaign=syndication.

23   Jessica Roy, "How Millennials Replaced Religion with Astrology and Crystals," *Los Angeles Times*, July 10, 2019, https://www.latimes.com/health/la-he-millennials-religion-zodiac-tarot-crystals-astrology-20190710-story.html.

24   Brenan, "Religiosity Largely Unaffected by Events of 2020 in U.S."

25   Pew Research Center, "Why America's 'Nones' Don't Identify with a Religion," Pew Research Center, July 23, 2020, https://www.pewresearch.org/fact-tank/2018/08/08/why-americas-nones-dont-identify-with-a-religion/.

26   Pew Research Center, "Political Polarization in the American Public," Pew Research Center, April 9, 2021, https://www.pewresearch.org/politics/2014/06/12/political-polarization-in-the-american-public/.

27   Judith Shulevitz, "The Lethality of Loneliness," *New Republic*, August 9, 2021, https://newrepublic.com/article/113176/science-loneliness-how-isolation-can-kill-you. For more, see Louise C. Hawkley and John T. Cacioppo, "Loneliness Matters: A Theoretical and Empirical Review of Consequences and Mechanisms," *Annals of Behavioral Medicine* 40, no. 2 (October 2010): 218–27, http://www.ncbi.nlm.nih.gov/pubmed/20652462.

28   Those who lack in means feel little freedom at all—and merit our immediate support.

29   Ian Carter, "Positive and Negative Liberty," Stanford Encyclopedia of Philosophy (Stanford University), August 2, 2016, https://plato.stanford.edu/entries/liberty-positive-negative/.

30   "Doxing Should Be Illegal. Reporting Extremists Should Not," Anti-Defamation League, January 15, 2021, https://www.adl.org/blog/doxing-should-be-illegal-reporting-extremists-should-not.

31   It is with gratitude that we credit our teacher Rabbi Brad Hirschfield with this key insight.

32   Pew Research Center, *Jewish Americans in 2020* (Washington, DC: Pew Research Center, May 14, 2021), https://www.pewforum.org/2021/05/11/jewish-americans-in-2020/.

33   Mark Oppenheimer, "Surprising Trends Driving Conversion to Judaism," *Tablet*, May 13, 2021, https://www.tabletmag.com/sections/community/articles/conversion-not-just-for-marriage-anymore.

34   Thomas G. Plante, "Are You Spiritually Homeless?," *Psychology Today*, April 12, 2010, https://www.psychologytoday.com/us/blog/do-the-right-thing/201004/are-you-spiritually-homeless.

Index

A

Aaron, 22, 34

Aaron Potek, 24, 145

Abraham, 7

Adon Olam, 10

advocacy, xvii-xviii, 31-32, 41, 45, 47, 78, 101-102, 131

affiliation, 13, 18, 78, 101, 109, 111, 148

Aish HaTorah, 5, 9, 45

Akiva, 47-48, 117, 136, 149

Alan Dershowitz, xiv, 139, 161

ALEPH: The Alliance for Jewish Renewal, 24, 115

American Israel Public Affairs Committee, 28

American Jewish Committee, xix, 28, 144, 147

American Jewish University, 16

Anti-Defamation League, xix, 28, 146-147, 162-163

antisemitism, xvi, 19, 21, 23, 27, 29, 42, 80, 90, 126, 129-131, 134, 140, 161

anti-Zionism, 78

apocalypse, xi

Ashkenazi, 137

assimilation, xiv-xv, 10, 25, 50, 129, 134, 139

B

Babchuck, Elan, xviii, 150, 160

Babel, 65

Babylonia, 50, 65

baby namings, 17, 72, 93

Baird, Justus, 80

Balaam, 22, 28

Balak, 22, 28

bat mitzvah, 10, 24, 43, 57, 150

beit din, 72

Berman, Amanda, 78, 139-140, 144, 155

Bernamoff, Noah, 5, 141

bikkur holim, 63

BimBam, 62-63, 152

Birthright Israel, 32, 48, 91, 147, 156

Black Lives Matter, 41

Bleicher, Jonah, 71

Borat, 23

Boycott, Divestment, Sanctions, 27

Breyer, Stephen, 113

Bromberg, Jodi, 93-94, 157

Buchdahl, Angela, 24, 145

Buddhism, 48

Bulliet, Richard, 118, 160

C

Campanella, Edoardo, 4, 141

Campbell, David, 22, 144

cantors, xix, 15, 17, 36, 64, 115, 141

Carlebach, Shlomo, 60, 151

Center for Rabbinic Innovation, 36

Center for Small Town Jewish Life, 107, 159

Chabad, 5, 25-26, 49, 60, 109-111, 145-146, 159

Chabon, Michael, 113

Chasidic, xxi, 9, 25, 97

chavruta, xxii, 123

Chicago, Judy, 113

CLAL, vii, 36, 97, 140, 148, 157-158, 160-161

clergy, xvii, xix, xxi, 5, 9, 11, 14, 16-19, 21, 23, 36, 47, 49, 58-60, 62-64, 72, 82, 84-86, 91, 93-96, 104, 107, 111, 113-115, 125, 142-143

Cohen, Sophia, 72

community centers, xvii, xx, 13, 101, 103

Congregation Beit Simchat Torah, 45

Culture and Child Protection

of related interest

Child Protection Work
Beyond the Rhetoric
Helen Buckley
ISBN 1 84310 075 4

Child Welfare Policy and Practice
Issues and Lessons Emerging from Current Research
Edited by Dorota Iwaniec and Malcolm Hill
ISBN 1 85302 812 6

Child Welfare Services for Minority Ethnic Families
The Research Reviewed
June Thoburn, Ashok Chand and Joanne Procter
Introduction by Beverley Prevatt Goldstein
ISBN 1 84310 269 2

Safeguarding and Promoting the Well-being of Children, Families and Communities
Edited by Jane Scott and Harriet Ward
Foreword by Maria Eagle MP
ISBN 1 84310 141 6

Developing Good Practice in Children's Services
Edited by Vicky White and John Harris
ISBN 1 84310 150 5

Children Taken Seriously
In Theory, Policy and Practice
Edited by Jan Mason and Toby Fattore
Foreword by Mary John
Children in Charge 12
ISBN 1 84310 250 1

Social Work Theories in Action
Edited by Mary Nash, Robyn Munford and Kieran O'Donoghue
Foreword by Jim Ife
ISBN 1 84310 249 8

Cultural Competence in the Caring Professions
Kieran O'Hagan
ISBN 1 85302 759 6